PRAISE FOR RUTH... ...

"*Ruthless Equity* is the most important book I've read in my 25 years in education. Ken's passion and purpose come to life and create a real call to action: to disrupt the status quo, crush complacency and make an impactful difference in our education system. This book is changing the trajectory of our school."
— Jove Stickel, Middle School Principal, Lafayette Co. C-1 Middle School

"In an era when the rhetoric around equity is increasingly abstract, Ken Williams demands that we make a choice: is our commitment to equity merely about saying the right words, or will it drive us to actually change the specific systems in our schools that stand in the way of equity for all?"
—Justin Baeder, Ph.D., author of *Now We're Talking!*
21 Days to High Performance Instructional Leadership

"It's finally here! A resource that is pure, honest, and real about doing what it takes to ensure real learning for all. This book needs to be in the hands of every public-school educator."
— Anisa Baker-Busby, Ed.D., Principal and Educational Consultant

"Equity is a word that is thrown around in education circles and in many cases the context and definition are inaccurate. Ken Williams sets the record straight. In this powerful book, he moves beyond the buzzword and focuses on actionable strategies to ensure that every learner regardless of zip code has access to an equitable learning culture. This book will make you uncomfortable, and also bump you up to make a greater difference in the lives of kids."
— Eric Sheninger, Google Certified Innovator, Adobe Education Leader

"*Ruthless Equity* is exactly what the educational world needs right now. While reading this book, I reflected on my own teaching practices and how I could become a better educator. I really enjoyed the end of chapter "disruptive action to take" section."
— Sean Daugherty, M. Ed., Kindergarten Teacher

"Ken Williams is the voice of reason heard loud and clear in an often-noisy conversation about equity. He clearly conveys that equity is not only a belief, but it also demands action. Equity is not achievable without a 'ruthless' commitment that is supported by policies, protocols, and processes aligning with the desire for equitable outcomes."
— Michael Walker, Assistant Director/Teacher Center Coordinator, Arkansas River Education Cooperative

"*Ruthless Equity* tackles equity in the K-12 context head on. It will make you laugh, make you uncomfortable, and help you see clearly where you can make equity a reality. With humor and heart-wrenching accounts, Ken makes it clear where educators should focus their time, energy, and attention: ensuring student learning for all kids. It is rare to find such a funny and shockingly real book aimed right at educators who are in the perfect position to put equity into practice."
— Brig Leane, Educational Consultant

"AHA, AMEN and NOW WHAT? As you read each chapter of *Ruthless Equity*, you will be made increasingly aware of the value inherent to each of these concepts. Thank you for stretching my thinking and validating the idea that making sure ALL kids master the essentials is the important work we do every day."
— JoAnne Greear, Principal, Jenifer Middle School

"Ken approaches the necessity of *Ruthless Equity* with a raw closeness and clarity of a practitioner who is in the trenches of the work. This book represents an unapologetic truth that taps into the root of issues that haunt and hinder education. Only the courageous stand firm to address the reality addressed by Ken Williams. *Ruthless Equity* demands that we as educators are relentless in our through-line."
— Marcus L. Broadhead, Ed.D., Educational Leader, Author, Speaker

"*Ruthless Equity* provides the hard-hitting necessary truths about equity or lack of equity in schools. Ken's radically candid approach will help you unearth and ameliorate equity issues in your district, school, and/or classroom. This book will not only inspire readers but will challenge all educators to check their own comfort in order to be ruthless in their own pursuit of equity for ALL!"
— Cory Radisch, educator, presenter, and co-host of The StatusGROW Podcast

"Thanks to Ken, I now have a new understanding of the two words Ruthless and Equity. Ken does not hold back and will push and stretch your thinking in fabulous new ways. I can't recommend this book highly enough for school teams wanting equitable practices to increase student learning."

— Bethany Brown, Principal, Buffalo Public Schools

Ruthless Equity is for any educator wrestling with the rhetoric around student equity. Ken Williams cuts right to the core of our practices — right into our districts, our schools, and our teams — to challenge the ambiguity around what equity is and what it is not. With clarity and practicality, Ken will challenge you to self-reflect and will push you into action to ensure high levels of learning for all students."

— Dani Trimble, Superintendent, Alburnett School District, Iowa

"Finally. Someone who gets that equity is more than buzzwords and slogans. Equity is about how we take action, and do the right work of ensuring high levels of learning for each and every student, each and every day, in each and every classroom. With humor that hits you up-side the head, stories that punch you in the gut, and logic that no one can defy, Ken shows us the way."

— Dr. Chad Dumas, author of *Let's Put the C in PLC: A Practical Guide for School Leaders*

"Are you ready to move from talking around equity to tackling equity in your schools? Then this is the book you need to read. Be ready to highlight, notate and talk about this book throughout the rest of your career."

— Jessica Cabeen, Nationally Distinguished Principal, NAESP Middle-Level Fellow, Author and Speaker (and Ken's biggest fan)

"In *Ruthless Equity*, Ken Williams offers an antidote to the institutional inertia, blame game, and 'window' effect that so many of us experience. This book is the resource we need to take equity work from ideal to real by outlining necessary shifts, eliminating excuses, and providing space for honest reflection and action planning."

—Dr. Alison J. Mello, Assistant Superintendent and Author

"Was I affirmed in my thinking and practices, or did I just get slapped out of my comfort zone? Ken Williams is not afraid to be authentic and bold. His heart is *ruthlessly* determined to inspire educators to an *urgent* place where students individually get what they need when they need it. Read this book and prepare for the desire to be a world changer."

— Dr. Felecia Spicer, Educational Leader

"*Ruthless Equity* is the book of all times for every educator seeking boldness in the classroom to dismiss the prescriptions written by society. Ken Williams has certainly parted the red sea of avoidance and cleared the path for reality. What's the reality? Equity for all!"

—Krystalyn E. May, Fifth Grade Teacher, Lindsey Elementary School

"*Ruthless Equity* is a brutally honest wake-up call for educators. With uncommon candor, Ken Williams moves the dialogue about equity away from national politics, educational policies and inspirational posters, and instead focuses relentlessly on what every educator can directly influence—the teaching practices and mindsets that advance or impede the success of our students. Ken challenges us to not only act upon his Four Rules of Ruthless Equity, but to courageously challenge those who actively—and passively—maintain the status quo. This book should leave you both uncomfortable and inspired."

— Mike Mattos, Educator, Author, Consultant

RUTHLESS
EQUITY

RUTHLESS EQUITY

**Disrupt the
Status Quo
and Ensure
Learning for
ALL Students**

KEN WILLIAMS

Ruthless Equity: Disrupt the Status Quo and Ensure Learning for ALL Students

Published by Wish in One Hand Press

To contact the author about booking talks, workshops, or bulk orders of this book, visit www.unfoldthesoul.com.

ISBN (paperback): 978-1-7379004-0-5
ISBN (ebook): 978-1-7379004-1-2

Editor: David Hogan
Book Design: Christy Day, Constellation Book Services,
www.constellatiobookservices.com

Printed in the United States of America

DEDICATION

This book is for my mother, Suzanne Williams. She passed away on January 25, 2021. If no one buys this book, I'll be disappointed, but I'll eventually sleep easy because I know she'd be proud of me for working past self-doubt and writing a solo-authored book. She'd be proud of me because I'm her son, and the manifestation of this goal is a direct reflection of her influence, values, and parenting.

CONTENTS

FOREWORD

Finally, a book for the tired! The marginalized members of societies all over the world are tired. Tired of what? Of waiting. Of conversations and stall tactics. We are at a point in history where we need to determine whether the old adage "All men are created equal" was a cruel deception or a promise that has slowly evolved and is on the precipice of becoming reality. The answers to these dilemmas greatly depend on the critical decisions that we make in this hour, at this time. Covid 19 has changed the world in ways we could never have imagined before the spring of 2020. This tipping point could shift our society toward the promise of its creed or send it spiraling down the rabbit hole of empty promises that has made our society a boiling cauldron. The choice lies with us.

Ruthless Equity is a bold attempt by Ken Williams to provide a roadmap to our higher angels. A book that is meant to not only inspire hope but also provide guidance, strategies, and concrete methodology to bring us closer to the promise of "liberty and justice for all." Our past has shown us, as Ken Williams states, "that we have to bet on ourselves." And our history has shown that schools that change lives pull from a strong, intrinsic sense of duty and humanity. The tired paths of Title I, Title II, IDEA, NCLB, and ESEA have proven that the government does not have the will or the skill to deliver on the promise of equity. And what about parents? Most are genuine and sincere, but the ever-increasing cost of living, stress of broken relationships, and strain of just trying to make ends meet in an increasingly less empathetic environment have rendered most parents of poverty impotent in their desire to see a better life for their children.

What is required to achieve the criteria of *Ruthless Equity*? It starts with a realization that education is a profession of service. It takes a realization that professional accomplishment is not thirty years of comfort and ease and the collection of a pension but involves doing the kind of work that transforms the lives of generations who will live long beyond your physical presence on this earth. It is using your craft to positively touch those whom this society has deemed irredeemable. It is restoring hope for those who've lost hope by the end of kindergarten. It requires a willingness to think differently and change the narrative. Skin color has no correlation to intelligence. English is not the only language on this planet. A disability does not equal inability. Poverty is a temporary life circumstance that can be overcome with the acquisition of a quality education.

I implore you and your colleagues to not just read this book but also digest each critical suggestion. We have a history of applauding great works such as *Pedagogy of the Oppressed* by Paulo Freire and then returning to our comfortable corners of apathy. This book is a mercy for those who have been comfortable talking about equity but are acting as barriers to its reality. That can't happen in this day and time; the masses are dissatisfied, and they want change and demand justice. Women grew weary of being objectified, harassed, and abused, and the "Me Too" movement cleaned house! African Americans grew tired of unjust police aggression, harassment, and violence, and Black Lives Matter swept the country. Are schools next? Will students, parents, and citizens who have felt neglected, underserved, ignored, and marginalized reach their boiling points?

History teaches us that the oppressed always have a reckoning with their oppressors. How have we acted oppressively? Many men and women of color remember pivotal moments in their school experience in which teachers or school administrators said things to them that crushed their spirit. Malcolm X vividly remembered a teacher telling him that "Negros don't become attorneys." The rapper The Notorious B.I.G., in his iconic track *Juicy*, dedicated the song to "all the teachers who told me that I would never amount to nothing!" This vitriolic mindset has led to lack of access and academic opportunity, disproportionate applications of punishment, huge graduation disparities, and a general sense of hopelessness in students of color and students from poverty.

Don't look at this book as an entertaining and enlightening analysis of inequity but as a professional playbook that is long overdue and that awards you a chance to shape history, not become a victim of it. Equity can never become reality in schools if we look at it through the lens of charity instead of professional obligation.

As you read this book, think of all those people who are tired. Whose lives can't wait another moment for you to get comfortable with their inclusion. Think of all those who have fought, marched, voted, and died for a place in this great society, and then realize that you can be the door to finally opening that reality to so many. No institution is in a better position to deliver on the promise of equity than public schools. Embrace that responsibility and be ruthless in your efforts to breathe life into every young person who is blessed to be a student at your school.

Dr. Anthony Muhammad
Author and Educational Consultant

WHAT I KNOW

The pursuit of equity for every student is going to expose you. It's going to tap into your fears and doubts. Your pursuit will simultaneously reveal your greatest strengths and shortcomings as an educator. Your fear of failure will be tested, the same fears associated with the risk of chasing your dreams because chasing your dreams *and* ensuring equity involve going for it!

Your self-worth as an educator will be tested. You will have to put your money where your mouth is. *Ruthless Equity* destroys all the numbing warmth provided by the "bell-shaped curse" and its false claim that you must sort your students into low, average, and high groups. Ensuring equity destroys excuses, the excuses that make you ache with "savior sympathy" (pity with charity). Pursuing equity doesn't ask, "What *can* you do?" but instead, "What are you *willing* to do?"

Understand this: There is no *passive* path to ensuring equity. Equity must be taken by force. It's more than changing policies and adopting new practices. There is an enemy in our midst, and its sole purpose is to create doubt in the service of protecting the status-quo. And while we all know it's a challenge for people to embrace change, systems double down and hate it even more. Systems have a tendency to protect themselves using rationalization, the manipulation of data, and sometimes even outright denial. The irony in our field is while education is the profession that creates all professions, in an ever-changing world, it is one of the most resistant systems to change.

The enemy has taken as its life's work coming up with unending ways to dismantle your efforts to embed equity. It will stop at nothing to do so. You will do battle with the enemy on a daily basis, and you must be ruthless. Ruthless Equity demands selfish excellence because there is a ruthlessness to excellence.

BOOK OVERVIEW

DOES THIS SOUND LIKE YOU?

- Does the inequity of "haves and have nots" secretly chip away at your confidence as an educator?
- Do you lose sleep wondering how to move equity from theory to instructional practices with positive impact?
- Are you fed up with equity initiatives that start on fire and eventually flame out with no tangible results?
- Do you have some colleagues who ensure equity for every student while other colleagues appear mired in dysfunction?
- Do you wake up dreading the thought that some of your teammates may not believe all students can learn at high levels?
- Do you secretly find yourself deeply frustrated and worn down by the excuses you've heard as to why students aren't learning?
- You know there's an urgent need for equity, but you're not sure how to ensure equity for all your students.
- I've come to know and work with so many educators who want to grow themselves and ensure equity and excellence for every student but are left stuck and overwhelmed in that pursuit thanks to:
  - ¤ The sudden emergence of brand-new "equity experts" who at best are guessing at what equity should look like in schools. They passionately identify problems while offering no practical solutions.
  - ¤ The sheer overabundance of information about equity makes the process of finding the right kind of guidance and solutions a mind-numbing experience.

¤ The non-stop rhetoric, clichés, and theories about equity that address everything except our fundamental purpose: ensuring every student masters essential learning outcomes.

- If these points read like I typed them using a hammer, you're getting a feel for how important ensuring equity has become for me.

- Ensuring a world class education to every student by leveraging the collective genius of educators, is the mission of this book.

LIFE IS TEN PERCENT WHAT HAPPENS TO YOU AND NINETY PERCENT HOW YOU REACT TO IT.
—CHARLES R. SWINDOLL

Boiled down to its simplest form, this book is written to help you understand three things:

1. The factors that accelerate equity in your classroom
2. The factors that impede equity in your classroom
3. The habits of mind and practice you must leverage to ensure equity for all students

So, while you may process situations that involve others, it's only and always about you. Let's explore how the book is organized.

OVERVIEW OF CHAPTERS

Chapter 1: Equity: The Right Thing Done the Wrong Way

One positive result to come out of the pandemic and social justice movement is how they have placed equity front and center in the national discussion around education. Simultaneously, one of the greatest frustrations in the emergence of equity is the abundance of rhetoric and misinformation around equity in schools. If you're a veteran educator, there's a part of you that expects this equity wave to come and go, with lots of energy and no tangible results. This has been the predictable pattern of equity initiatives.

Doing the research for this book has helped me better understand my struggle with diversity efforts. I have clarity, and no longer aspire to have diversity be a goal. My intent isn't to dishonor the time, energy, effort, and sacrifice of people who've led diversity efforts. But, when I consider the results of diversity efforts, I've come to the conclusion that they are more *surface* than *substance*. Again, I'm not disparaging the effort. The intention of diversity initiatives is to get beneath the surface and connect with substance, but time after time, they fail to do so.

You'll discover the missing elements that will make equity sustainable and not a fad.

Chapter 2: Radioactive Rhetoric

There is an enemy poised to completely sabotage every move you make and risk you take in the service of ensuring equity for all students. The enemy takes no time off. It's on the clock 24/7, just like the Queen's Guard at Buckingham Palace, baby. I'm going to introduce this equity killer and help you recognize the many forms it takes.

Chapter 3: Ruthless Equity

You'll begin training with the weapon you'll use to defeat the enemy. You'll learn why you must be ruthless in your mission to ensure equity, excellence, and achievement for all students, regardless of background. You'll finish this chapter with a new perspective on ruthlessness, and you'll be introduced to The Four Rules of Ruthless Equity.

Chapter 4: Ruthless Rule 1: A Commitment to Courage Over Comfort

Who doesn't want change for the better? Disrupting the status-quo sounds good rolling off the tongue, and it sure looks enticing from a distance. But in reality, we prefer not to stand out or work in ways that are counter to the majority. With this in mind, I want to prepare you for what to expect from yourself and what to be aware of in others when you work for change. Disrupting the status-quo takes courage, and you'll be more empowered once you understand the price of admission.

Chapter 5: Ruthless Rule 2: A Commitment to Dismantling Ability Groups

Ability groups and tracking are inequitable practices. Ability groups and every other tracking policy and practice must be dismantled and eradicated. In this chapter, I'll explain why the practice is inequitable and provide you with a viable equitable alternative.

Chapter 6: Ruthless Rule 3: A Commitment to Start with the Crown

You're more courageous. You look around and see the collective genius in your colleagues. Now it's time to learn about the habits of mind and practice that define Ruthless Equity. This chapter highlights equitable practice. All practicality and no ambiguity!

Chapter 7: Ruthless Rule 4: A Commitment to Momentum Over Mood Rings

No status-quo, mission-driven, learning-for-all pursuit is immune to challenges, frustrations, and false starts. In this chapter, I meet you at the door with a box of what you should expect and how to respond to potential problems of all kinds. This way, you'll pierce the barrier that thwarts the efforts of so many and position yourself for awesome learning breakthroughs.

Chapter 8: You Must DE-CIDE

Now it's time take action. Your ruthless equity lens has provided you with the opportunity to examine your existing classroom, team, and school culture. This chapter provides a new definition of the word, decide. This definition will aide you in deciding what you will start doing, stop doing, and continue doing in the service of ensuring equity. What will you dismantle and disrupt in the service of learning excellence for each one of your students? This is where the rubber meets the road, baby.

End of Chapter: Disruptive Engagement

To disrupt the status-quo, you've got to do more than read, you've got to engage. Each chapter will provide an opportunity for you to reflect on the text and how it will inform both your mindset and practice. Chapters will close with a list of "Ruthless Key Points" to remember, followed by "Disruptive Actions to Take." Don't skip this step. Remember, there is no *passive* path to *Ruthless Equity*.

STREAMING VIDEO CLIPS

One of the best parts about this resource is that it includes micro-learning video clips of Ken bringing selected topics to life through streaming video. The videos are there to help you understand the concepts better. Use them to enhance your own learning experience with the content. You can use them with others to spark conversation inside your book study and with colleagues and teammates. This video content is available through QR codes. To read a QR code, you must have a smartphone or tablet with a camera. We recommend you download a QR reader app that is made specifically for your phone or tablet brand.

Videos may also be accessed at:
www.youtube.com/unfoldthesoul

Search: Ruthless Equity Videos
Or you can scan this code

USING THIS TEXT AS A BOOK STUDY

This text is designed for both **group and individual learning**. Each chapter provides opportunities to reflect, write, engage, and take action. Here's where I need you to be both mindful and careful. Many of the passages in this text are going to bring you head-on into challenging situations, colleagues who've behaved poorly, and times when you've been treated poorly. With the wrong lenses, you're going to have plenty of content to fuel gossip and relive personal instances when you were victimized. If you're wearing those lenses now, take them off and clean them.

No matter the experiences and memories this text triggers for you, know that in the end, it always comes back to *you: your* choices, *your* responses, what *you* learn, *your* mindset, *your* influence, *your* impact, and *your* results.

So, while you may process situations that involve others, it's only and always about *you.*

WHAT I NEED YOU TO KNOW

Educators are amazing! Education is the profession that creates all professions. Education is among the noblest of professions. There, I said it. And I mean it. I wouldn't have written this book if I didn't. With that said, hear this: When a coach reviews the game film with players, he doesn't spend seventy-five of the ninety-minute session highlighting excellent plays. Great coaches spend some time celebrating what the team did well, and more time identifying areas for improvement. With that in mind, regard this book as game film. Refer to the quote at the top of the page for the celebration. Take it in, because we're going to spend most of our time identifying opportunities to get better.

So, if you need me to blow warm sunshine off your back every four pages regarding how amazing educators are, their thankless plight, and other ineffective platitudes, I am not your author, and this is not your book. Find the receipt you just tossed and return the book for a refund. Or use it as fire-pit kindling, toilet paper, or perhaps to stabilize your wobbly dining room table. Then, walk to your bookshelf, close your eyes, reach out, and grab any five books from your shelf written for educators. Sit down and turn to any random page in each book. Chances are, you'll get all the warm and fuzzy validation you're looking for.

On the other hand, if you understand that moving from "learning for *some*" to "equity for *all*" involves an unvarnished and honest examination of how you must be better, *Ruthless Equity* is for you. Because you understand that greatness involves the willingness to take a cold, hard stare at what's not working, and embracing the challenge to improve in those areas. If you want to have a career of significance, influence, and impact, you must be willing to do what most others won't, which is: owning the conditions around you. Mediocre educators see owning as a burden. Ruthless educators understand that owning is the very source of their power.

I am grateful for this time in our history where equity is on the radar of school districts. I also understand the pendulum swings in education that treat issues like trends that come and go. I was hesitant to write this book because of my fear of this issue fading away.

> WE ARE RESPONSIBLE FOR WHAT WE ARE AND WHATEVER WE WISH OURSELVES TO BE. WE HAVE THE POWER TO MAKE OURSELVES. IF WHAT WE ARE NOW HAS BEEN THE RESULT OF OUR OWN PAST ACTIONS, IT CERTAINLY FOLLOWS THAT WHATEVER WE WISH TO BE IN THE FUTURE CAN BE PRODUCED BY OUR PRESENT ACTIONS; SO, WE HAVE TO KNOW HOW TO ACT.
> —VIVEKANANDA

Greatness is born of being stretched, challenged, and provoked; it comes from having the status-quo disrupted, your paradigms shifted, and your curiosity piqued. And who you will become for students will be life-changing. Your impact will be immeasurable. I want students to lose count of how many great educators make a significant, positive impact in their life. Today, we know this isn't the case for most students, but tomorrow can be different. For that to happen, you must submit to being coached, and coached hard.

There's a secret ruthless educators know that other educators don't, and the secret is this: It's not the execution of practice that's challenging. What's challenging is committing one's heart, head, and hands to the mission of executing the principles of *Ruthless Equity* relentlessly and consistently. Everyone wants to make equity happen for all students (heart), everyone can make a culture of equity make sense theoretically (head), but not everyone is willing to commit to doing (hands). The force that keeps us from this level of commitment is Complacency.

Grabbing your heart, head, and hands isn't good enough. *I want your soul.*

WHAT ARE ESSENTIAL LEARNING OUTCOMES?

I'm going to reference essential learning outcomes throughout this book because ensuring that every student masters them is the primary measurable indicator of equitable practice. Schools and districts may use a variety of different terms for essential learning outcomes, such as priority standards, essential standards, need-to-knows, power standards, non-negotiable standards, and others.

In Chapter 3 of the book, *Concise Answers To Frequently Asked Questions About Professional Learning Communities At Work*, Mike Mattos and his coauthors offer this explanation: *Essential standards* identify the knowledge, skills, and dispositions all students must acquire as a result of a class, course, or grade-level. Essential standards go beyond what is nice to know and identify what students *must* know to be proficient. Students and teachers benefit from a focused, cohesive, and well-articulated curriculum. By agreeing on what is essential, teachers take a significant and fundamental first step toward equipping their students to learn.

Ensuring mastery of essential learning outcomes is different from merely covering the standards. Ensuring learning involves teaching the student, and not just the standard. There are no exceptions in the definition. Regardless of student background and circumstance, the mission of teachers is to determine how to reach every student in the service of mastery of essential learning outcomes. As you continue to read this book, you'll learn why being ruthless is a vital component to your success as a teacher.

WE CAN, WHENEVER AND WHEREVER WE CHOOSE, SUCCESSFULLY TEACH ALL CHILDREN WHOSE SCHOOLING IS OF INTEREST TO US. WE ALREADY KNOW MORE THAN WE NEED TO DO THIS. WHETHER WE DO IT OR NOT MUST FINALLY DEPEND ON HOW WE FEEL ABOUT THE FACT THAT WE HAVE NOT DONE IT SO FAR.

—DR. RON EDMONDS, THE FATHER OF EFFECTIVE SCHOOLS RESEARCH

CHAPTER ONE

EQUITY INITIATIVES: THE RIGHT THING DONE THE WRONG WAY

OUR DYSFUNCTIONAL DANCE

THE DYSFUNCTIONAL CYCLE OF EQUITY WORK

1. **"Catalyst!"** Something draws a school's/district's attention to inequity. Some catalyst brings significant attention to issues of race, racism, equity, and access.

2. **"We believe in equity for every student."** In response to the catalyst, a school or district leader makes a public commitment to equity. "We believe in equity" or "This [inequity] isn't who we are" are familiar statements.

3. **"Let's form a committee to lead the effort."** The school/district then moves from the public pronouncement to starting a committee. District leadership directs a group of equity-passionate individuals to convene with the goal of making the public declaration actionable. Whether they are teachers, teacher-leaders, or assistant principals, these people rarely have the positional authority or technical expertise to bring about real change. The committee decides that the equity initiative requires training for staff.

4. **"I know someone who can help."** Because equity-passionate is not the same as equity-competent, the committee

discovers its limitations in capacity and expertise. The committee members need help. The group needs an outside speaker/consultant who uses an attractive, en vogue approach. Upon its completion, some educators feel validated, while others—usually White and/or those who are well-served by the current structure—leave feeling uneasy, offended, or even blamed. Negative conversations happen in private, and rumors spread.

5. **"We're (re)starting the conversation."** After the consultant leaves, the training program becomes the responsibility of the original committee. This group often assumes a train-the-trainer stance and attempts to recreate the experience for others. However, the committee still hasn't developed the capacity to hold the space for critical conversations, nor have they developed the expertise in content or transformative process. Although equity-passionate educators cheer on the committee, others do not.

6. **"Why aren't we seeing anything change?"** As time passes after the training, dismay begins to grow across the organization. Those who were offended by the training retreat into small groups where they can commiserate quietly amongst themselves about the initiative. Those who were supportive grow frustrated by the lack of strategy and follow-up to the event. Dismayed by the fact that they are still witnessing the type of harmful behaviors and statements that led to the equity initiative, they raise their voices: "Why isn't anything changing?"

7. **"Let's focus on something practical and not so esoteric."** As the pressure for results increases, people scurry in an effort to answer these cries for help and demands for accountability. Someone with influence inevitably suggests focusing on the classroom and an equity pedagogy.

The leadership team then trains or directs teachers in the approach, hoping that these efforts will bring about the needed change.

8. **"Just tell us what you want us to do and we'll do it."** The training leaves many participants feeling confused by the esoteric nature of the concept. Frustration grows, and even educators committed to the effort plead for a list of practical strategies for the classroom.

9. **"It's just good teaching, after all."** Due to the lack of a prescriptive course of action with the equity pedagogy, many teachers rationalize inaction by reducing things to "effective instruction." They focus on an existing aspect of practice— such as cooperative learning. Soon thereafter the teachers relegate the equity initiative to just "one more thing."

10. **"Remember when we used to focus on this type of thing**? The status-quo remains firmly intact. The espoused commitment to equity does not translate into equity in action. The equity initiative quietly fades away and attention shifts to other matters. That is, until another catalyst occurs and returns us to Step 1.

Adapted from *Belonging Through a Culture of Dignity* by Cobb and Krownapple.

This synopsis of Cobb and Krownapple's findings outline the typical pattern so many schools and districts experience. The accuracy of this cycle stopped me in my tracks. I've seen the pattern so many times. I've always chalked it up to the pendulum swings we experience in education. I'm grateful to the authors for investing time and energy into researching equity work.

As a speaker, there are few things more satisfying than when you share something that reveals how well you know your audience. It's those moments when you see the road ahead, know where they've been, or say exactly what they're thinking. I liken it to the transformation that occurs when the door-to-door salesperson you're wary of says something that gets him invited to sit at your kitchen table. When I see my audience have that moment, I know I'm *in your kitchen, baby.*

I write this knowing exactly how my audience feels when I'm in their kitchen, because Floyd Cobb and John Krownapple, authors of *Belonging Through a Culture of Dignity,* are in my kitchen as I write this! I recommend their book, and will reference information from their work to make your next moves toward equity for all practical and meaningful. But they dig into so much more around equity initiatives, how they start, and why most of them fail. They break down the dysfunctional cycle of equity initiative implementation in the same way my co-author, Tom Hierck and I break down the dysfunctional mission statement creation process in our book, *Starting a Movement; Building Culture from the Inside-Out in Professional Learning Communities.* It matters not where your school is located, you will connect with the typical cycle of equity implementation so, you may want to sweep the kitchen floor and load the dishwasher, because company is coming over.

Reflect on your past experiences with equity-focused initiatives.

What were the strengths of the initiative?

....

....

....

What were the weaknesses of the initiative?

....

....

....

To what degree did the equity initiative result in significant change in your classroom, school, or district?

Cobb and Krownapple outline the typical pattern so many schools and districts experience. The authors conclude:

> ## EQUITY PASSIONATE DOESN'T MAKE ONE EQUITY COMPETENT.
> ### —COBB AND KROWNAPPLE

PLEASE WALK VS. DON'T RUN!

When I refer to "that school" in this book and in my videos, know that the phrase is based on the last school I led as principal. At the time, our school was the worst-performing in a district labeled as one of the worst in the greater Atlanta area. The culture was chaotic. Student behavior reflected that chaos. Part of our vision was to change the feel of our hallways. At the time, students were racing up and down the hallways. It was out of control. Staff members could be heard constantly screaming and shouting, "stop running!" or "don't run!" To this end, we made what looked on paper to be an almost imperceptible change. To change student behavior in our hallways, we made the decision to say to students: "please walk" instead of "don't run." Our rationale was simple. We decided it would be more impactful to "speak to the expected behavior," and redirecting student behavior with the phrase, "please walk" accomplished that, while it also curtailed the undesirable behavior. The process of transforming our school culture and results involved creating a shared vision. In our book, *Starting a Movement*, Tom and I named the second stage of the Authentic Alignment framework, The Eye: The process of creating a clear and compelling vision of the school you seek to become.

Part of this process involved assessing our current reality, our history, points of pride, regret, perceptions, reality, and legacy. We unearthed everything. We brought every issue into the light, with the intent of discussing and deciding if it's something we want to keep, change, or get rid of. It resulted in powerful discussions and a long list of:

- what we didn't want
- what we would no longer accept or tolerate
- behaviors we wanted to eradicate
- things we needed to stop doing
- things students needed to stop doing
- negative perceptions we wanted to shed
- negative student learning results we wanted to change

This stage of the process was necessary and cathartic. There was no way we could move forward and co-create a new culture without bringing these issues to the surface. These were all the things we were against continuing at our school. You could say we were: anti-a lot of things. This stage was necessary, but it alone didn't create any sustainable change. I'm proud to say that this was a rare instance when I knew we needed to go further than identifying what we didn't want. I knew that our only chance of sustained success was to now engage staff in getting as specific about what we did want.

In our book, *Starting a Movement*, Tom and I identify three levels of visioning:

- The **Inspiration** stage brings a realization that we are part of something larger than ourselves, and we have among us the gifts, talents, and tools to transform our school's culture.
- The **Aspiration** stage sees you progress from what you don't want to do to what you *do* want to do.

- The **Perspiration** stage involves getting to work to make shared aspirations a reality.

Nothing changed until we got clear on desired outcomes that were aspirational and stated in the affirmative. This isn't Pollyanna "just be positive" junk. This approach speaks to how our brains work and how we manifest results as human beings. If we never get around to envisioning a future that's better than our current reality, our efforts in any endeavor will fall short of the mark. We are much more powerful when we *stand for something* rather than *being against something.*

Many well-intentioned equity initiatives have their GPS set to arrive at *Fallen Short Avenue* because they're rooted solely in negative/ "anti" outcomes:

- anti-racism
- anti-bias
- dismantling White Supremacy
- eliminating micro-aggressions

Racism is an institutionalized system of social exclusion within which people and institutions use race to determine belonging and access. It's rooted in *power over others.* In schools, ability grouping or academic tracking is a policy and practice with staying power beyond comprehension. Academic tracking is the practice of separating students by academic ability within a school.

Jeanne Oakes, of UCLA conducted groundbreaking research in the area of tracking, which proved the practice to be ineffective for all students in general, and especially for students sentenced to lower tracks. This practice inevitably devolves into a system of exclusion along racial lines, within which "so called minority" students, especially students of color, are more likely to end up in lower-level tracks. What gets my blood boiling is not only the fixed mindset present in this practice, but the fact that standardized tests don't measure intelligence at all. It measures content knowledge, which requires access. And in a tracking system, access is denied, and the cycle continues.

Oakes and many others found that when schools dismantled tracking practices:

- Many teachers successfully worked with heterogeneous groups, boosting the achievement of under-served students above what it would have been in tracked classes;
- Higher-achieving students did just as well in heterogeneous classes;
- Racial gaps in enrollment in challenging courses were reduced, significantly in some cases.

These results are compelling, and should lead to dismantling this destructive inequitable practice. But these sobering facts have proved no match for three deep seated beliefs and norms that envelop education in our country:

1. Beliefs about ability to learn being finite or fixed: you either have it, or you don't; based on perceived genetic dominance, the bell-shaped curve, culture, or race;
2. Fear and hostility associated with racial and social-class mixing;
3. The politics of power where families with means use school ranking and success as a means to maintain the status-quo, which is to be protected as they pass advantages down to their next generation.

I have yet to introduce the word *ruthless* in the context of this work, but I bet you're beginning to get an idea of what ruthless equity means. You are up against a system that promotes and supports inequity by design. These are cultural norms that are sustained, nourished, promoted, and supported. Fixing inequality isn't neuroscience, and not fixing it is a deliberate choice.

Aside from academic tracking, the other issues are real as well, and need to be addressed. I find it curious how the "anti-issue" movement has welcomed issues using terms created in the past year. We're creating new "anti" issues while consciously avoiding the "anti-tracking" issues prevalent at most schools throughout North America. It's a cleverly engineered distraction designed to protect the status-quo.

There's another problem with equity initiatives focusing primarily on issues schools should stop doing. Equity movements driven by being against something don't inspire aspiration, vision, and clarity of direction. Frank Dobbin, co-author of the article, "Are Diversity Programs Merely Ceremonial?" revealed that professional development focused solely on diversity or anti-bias trainings doesn't result in change for the better. He goes further, citing that many initiatives produce negative results: further inequity, hardened attitudes toward equity, disappointed expectations, damaged relationships among colleagues, and backlash against those members of marginalized identities.

Movements rooted in negative outcomes don't provide a vision of a better tomorrow. Without the aspirational component, these well-intentioned efforts manifest a universal truth: negative energy produces negative results.

The phrase *please walk* in place of *don't run* addressed the undesirable behavior and created a vision to which to aspire. While this may seem an innocuous example, we applied the same thinking to everything we did at the school, and the difference it made was game changing. The same principle applies to today's equity initiatives. Movements rooted in "anti-anything" must create space for creating a clear vision of a better future. Absent that vision, it'll be doomed to land on the growing heap of failed equity initiatives.

To what extent have your equity efforts included an aspirational shared vision?

THE MISSING LINKS

I've always known how important it is for students to feel valued and seen. Creating a sense of belonging is paramount to learning success. Cobb and Krownapple focus on students, but the principle applies to humans as a species. The authors identify three overlooked areas that serve as the keys to success in equity work; inclusion, belonging, and dignity. They assert: "We believe that these keys have not been identified and understood, or they've been falsely assumed, undervalued, or ignored. For equity initiatives to succeed, we believe that educators must focus on shaping inclusive environments intentionally designed to foster a sense of belonging by honoring the dignity of each and every person."

THE UNWELCOMED

In my work with schools and districts, I often acknowledge the challenge of creating a culture of equity and belonging *inside* schools, while *outside*, our country grapples with coming to terms with a history of inequity. The hard truth is; unwelcoming environments where certain people are seen as not belonging (unwelcome) is part of our legacy yesterday and our current reality today.

In his article, "8 Reasons You Feel Like You Don't Belong Anywhere," author, Jack Nollan describes *not belonging* as a feeling of complete rejection of who you are because if nobody likes you for who you are or 'gets' you, it's hard not to take it personally. There have been times in my life when I've stood out in a room like black pepper on a mound of snow, and felt all the awkwardness you can imagine. Almost as if there's a neon sign running on fresh batteries attached to my chest. I've also had experiences when I've walked into a room of the same racial makeup and I'm made to feel at home. I can be my authentic self, which makes the racial optics an observation, and nothing more.

Feeling unwelcome is not limited to race and ethnic culture. There are so many factors present in an organization that can move the needle between belonging and unwelcome, that it's critical that you're aware of the power of belonging, and intentional about creating the conditions that make your students feel connected.

One of the missing keys to sustaining an equity initiative is to learn how to create positive, inclusive environments. As Cobb and Krownapple put it, "climates of belonging through cultures of dignity. In these environments, equity can take root and flourish." Inclusion, belonging, and dignity are the overlooked aspects of culture needed to break the repeated cycle of well-intentioned but failed equity initiatives.

THE DANGER OF DIVERSITY

As a Black man in America, I've always had an uneasy relationship with efforts to increase diversity. I could never put my finger on exactly what the solution was, but I am in touch with how I felt about it. I understood the good intentions behind diversity, and at times, I've celebrated them. And yet, something still was unsettled in my soul. While feeling pride by breaking barriers, there is nothing worse than wondering if access to an opportunity is based on merit or on quota. Well, maybe there is something worse, and that is when access is based on merit, but the general perception of others is that it wasn't. Instead, perhaps it was based on race, culture, or gender.

The "belonging" that diversity initiatives create feel forced. Instead of a real exploration behind why there's a lack of representation, diversity efforts often boil down to "increasing numbers" or achieving a "quota," which on the surface provides the optics of progress, but really don't tap into the substance that transforms school culture. Long term, they do more harm than good as they provide fertile soil for angst, resentment, doubt, insecurity, and over-compensation, among other issues.

Consider some of the diversity-based statements broached by schools and districts across the country:

- "We need more Black students in gifted programs."
- "We need more girls in science and engineering."

- "We need more underserved students taking Advanced Placement courses"
- "We need to reduce the number of suspensions of Black boys."
- "We need fewer Black students referred to Special Education."

Humbly, I now say, diversity cannot be our goal. I'm humble because I have evolved and can empathize with many who still believe this is the most positive path to change. It isn't. While well intentioned, addressing these issues has resulted in reducing people to symbols, objects and numbers. Cobb and Krownapple state that these statements view identity as a commodity that can be selected and consumed without considering the climate and the lack of belonging that produced the numbers.

We've been lulled to sleep by the intentions of diversity efforts, numbed by forced outcomes that appear to be positive results. Rather than explore root causes that contribute to inequitable situations, diversity efforts address the issue cosmetically, while solving nothing. Instead of dealing with the bias associated with the percentage of black boys referred for special education services, we simply refer fewer boys. Instead of exploring the reasons why more students of color aren't taking advanced courses, we simply place more students in those classes.

These examples are two sides of the same coin. We move on from these issues based on the look of things, rather than exploring the layers beneath them; and while numbers are shifted, mindsets are not. And still living beneath the surface response is the status-quo, unchanged and stronger than ever. The reality is, diversity does not ensure belonging.

Along with equitable instructional practices, Ruthless Equity requires that you get beneath the surface to address issues around belonging. It should aspire to create a culture where every student and every staff member feels appreciated, validated, accepted, and treated fairly; a culture where every student is provided what they need, when they need it, with urgency, to ensure mastery of essential learning outcomes. This is easier said than done because the impetus for change isn't the burden of those who come to us. It's on us.

INCLUSION AND BELONGING

Equity initiatives focus a lot on access. The phrase, "equity and access" are joined together so often that it's almost become a compound word. But, like diversity efforts, a focus on access alone will lead us down the same path of symbolism and surface results. We have to also explore how we got here, and how to create a culture where access has as its foundation, authentic inclusion and belonging.

Recall a situation when you felt like you did not belong.

What indicators signaled a lack of belonging?

What feelings did you experience?

How did the situation affect your level of engagement?

Equity and a Sense of Belonging

Guiding Question: How are you intentional about creating a culture of belonging in your classroom?

In educational parlance, *inclusion* can take on multiple contexts and meanings. For the sake of clarity, I'm not referring to inclusion in the context of students receiving special education support. In the context of creating a culture of equity, inclusion involves us examining all existing forms of diversity in our classroom and at our school, and shaping the culture to welcome and honor differences.

Inclusion is about what we change to create a welcoming environment. We do this to make everyone feel that they belong because of their differences, not in spite of them. This approach opens the way for everyone to feel a sense of belonging. Everyone feels seen, valued, and honored. They feel welcome. This is the birthplace of community. And once established, everyone feels a sense of investment in co-creating the culture. As Cobb and Krownapple put it, "Inclusion is about people partnering with one another to change the culture so that everyone experiences access and unconditional belonging."

INCLUSION IS NOT A STRATEGY TO HELP PEOPLE FIT INTO THE SYSTEMS AND STRUCTURES WHICH EXIST IN OUR SOCIETIES; IT IS ABOUT TRANSFORMING THOSE SYSTEMS AND STRUCTURES TO MAKE IT BETTER FOR EVERYONE. INCLUSION IS ABOUT CREATING A BETTER WORLD FOR EVERYONE. —DIANE RICHLER, PAST PRESIDENT, INCLUSION INTERNATIONAL

One of the points that struck me in my research on the necessity of belonging in equity initiatives is how much it's overlooked and, when not overlooked, how often schools gloss over the idea, assuming it's already embedded in their culture. You cannot achieve equity without this component. The purpose of this section is to provide you with questions to activate your thinking about the best next steps to achieve students' sense of belonging. These questions can be applied to all levels of the organization; from individual classroom teacher, collaborative team, the school, and the district.

A Culture of Belonging: An Inventory to Assess Your Current Reality
With a team of colleagues, reflect, record, and react to the following questions.

1. How do we know the extent to which students and staff members feel they belong to our school?
2. If we don't know, how can we begin to measure belonging and disaggregate our data?
3. How can we work with intentionality to nurture a sense of belonging for all students?
4. What do we need to continue doing?
5. What do we need to stop doing?
6. What do we need to start doing?
    a. By when?
    b. Who will be responsible for next steps?

Cobb, Floyd; Krownapple, John. *Belonging Through a Culture of Dignity: The Keys to Successful Equity Implementation.* Mimi & Todd Press, Inc. Kindle Edition.

SIMPLE, POWERFUL, AND SOBERING

I'll offer questions to provide you an opportunity to reflect on these issues and get dialogue started. In addition to the questions, I'm going to share one practical protocol that you can put into practice tomorrow.

It's a protocol that I've always known to be effective, but admittedly, didn't realize how effective until I dove into the research done by Cobb and Krownapple.

The authors cite a study done by Dr. Clayton Cook. Cook and his research team devised a protocol they named, Positive Greetings at the Door (PGD). They conducted the most comprehensive study of this type. Here are the 5 steps to the PGD protocol:

1. Stand or sit at or around your classroom door.
2. Positively connect with each student by saying each person's name and incorporating a verbal or nonverbal greeting (e.g., student choice of a hug, high five, fist-bump, or wave).
3. Ask each student how their day has started and make positive "pre-corrective" statements that presume a healthy start to the day and encourage agreed-upon guidelines for behavior.
4. Privately encourage students who had struggled with behavior the previous day.
5. Deliver behavior-specific praise.

The study was done using two control groups. Ten middle school teachers who started each class by implementing the PGD protocol with fidelity, and ten who started each class with no protocol in particular.

The results of the study showed great results! There was a twenty percent increase in academic engagement and a nine percent decrease in disruptive classroom behaviors. Going a layer deeper with the data revealed that a teacher could potentially add an extra hour of academic engagement per school day. This extra hour isn't a result of an extended school day. The hour is a result of students feeling valued and seen. This one simple protocol increases feelings of inclusion and belongingness. It fosters dignity, and it's free! It doesn't require extra training or financial investment. It simply requires awareness, intention, commitment, and consistency.

I found the positive results of this study to be simultaneously encouraging and sobering. I'm encouraged because this protocol is available to every educator, every school, and every district regardless of budget. I find it sobering because as educators, we cannot turn away from the questions it forces us to face:

- Why are these practices not the norm in our schools?
- Why do educators not use these techniques with students, all the time?

Nicole Williams is a 5th grade teacher at Burch Elementary. I affectionately refer to her as the Pied Piper of Burch. She's the kind of teacher every student would be blessed to have. She's as much a student as she is a teacher. She's a warm demander, relational, collaborative, and lives to unearth the strengths and gifts in every student. Every day of her more than 20 years as a teacher begins at the door of her classroom. She makes it a priority to warmly greet every student, every day, without fail. She has always gotten along well with teammates, but they've all come to learn that when students arrive, collegial conversation stops because it's time to roll out the red carpet for students.

Word must travel fast with students because it wasn't long before students in other grades who passed her classroom on the way to their own classroom began stopping by for that warm morning greeting. Somehow, the word got out among Burch's pre-k students, and a sizable delegation of 4- and 5-year-old students made the daily visit to the doorway of her classroom for their greeting and hug, which often led to them wanting her to notice new clothes, shoes, and hairstyles. Nicole refers to them as *my little friends,* and before long, some of her little friends would offer compliments and feedback on Nicole's fashion choices, hairstyles, and anything else they happen to notice.

Nicole Williams happens to be my beautiful wife, so I've seen this phenomenon happen in real time. I've watched as many of her little friends eventually become her 5th grade students. Students cycle through and new little friends are born. All of this, the result of making greeting students at the door a priority. Nicole is ruthless about extending dignity and fostering belongingness to every one of her students (and many others), every day. I'm proud of her, and I know other teachers make greeting students at the door a priority. Nicole and other teachers who make this a daily priority stand out as exceptional. But should this be exceptional? More importantly for educators to consider, Why is this example exceptional for educators?

Wrestling with this question has me reflecting on my tenure as a school leader, and many tense conversations with teachers about implementing the daily school-wide practice of greeting every student as they entered the classroom. I had no awareness of Cobb and Krownapple's research at the time. It just made sense to me that greeting students at the door increased the likelihood of a positive start to the day. It was a way to take the pulse of students who might be dealing with issues brought to school from home.

One of the outcomes of our shared vision was to have every student know that someone at our school was happy they showed up today. And while some teachers followed this practice already, too many others pushed back against the idea. They felt put upon. It was regarded at one school as another "duty," which often resulted in it devolving into a mere act of compliance, and worse, an act of defiant compliance. Students are perceptive. I'm certain they picked up on which teachers greeted them sincerely, and which ones did it because they *had to*.

I also own the possibility that I didn't explain the "why" of the expectation clearly enough. Again, I knew it was good practice, I knew it would strengthen our culture, but I didn't know then what I now know about its impact on creating a culture of equity. Cobb and Krownapple uncover a truth that's difficult to face: as a field, educators do not honor dignity as a normalized practice.

If you recoiled reading that statement, know that you're not alone. I did as well. My first reaction was defensive. We didn't enter education to look past people, violate the dignity of individuals, or create conditions that make students feel unwelcome. We got into this to help students, to inspire them, and to mine for their strengths in the service of learning. If you create space to reflect on that statement, it's difficult not to acknowledge that dignity violations are more normal than dignity honored. This situation is less an indictment of individual educators than it is an alarm that sounds a warning about the power of school culture.

Culture is the foundation of everything we do. It's the soil from which our decisions, policies, and practices grow. Culture shapes our behavior. Cobb and Krownapple assert, "Our culture has normalized dignity violations, indicated by the way it privileges achievement of social and academic standards over belonging. We can disrupt the status-quo, and dismantle the existing hierarchy that causes many of us to either not see those we serve or look down on "others" who we perceive to be beneath us.

Learning more requires a commitment to doing better, and becoming the best version of ourselves. And we can start with this protocol. Make the commitment to be more intentional about creating a culture that welcomes students, teammates, and everyone who enters your learning space. Let them know you see them, value them, and appreciate them.

RUTHLESS REMINDERS

- Educational equity requires a commitment to access and belonging.
- A sense of belonging is a fundamental human desire, so we have to ask ourselves why we do not prioritize it. We must admit our complicity in the perpetuation of this form of inequity.
- Belonging and inclusion are two overlooked keys to successful equity implementation.
- Racism is a system of social exclusion within which people and institutions use markers of race to determine belonging.
- In schools, academic tracking is a system of exclusion that devolves along racial lines within which students of color are more likely to end up in lower-level tracks.
- Many equity initiatives focus attention on what we *don't want* (anti-racism/anti-bias), rather than what we do want.

- "Anti" initiatives are well-intentioned, but risk negative results due to a lack of shared aspirational outcomes.
- There is greater power in being *for* something rather than being *against* something.
- Inclusion requires the community to evolve and transform to promote a sense of belonging. It affirms the talents, culture, strengths, backgrounds and beliefs of all its members.

DISRUPTIVE ACTIONS TO TAKE

With a team of colleagues, reflect, answer, and discuss the following questions/prompts:

1. Describe a time when you felt the need to change or hide something about yourself, to conform, or to achieve something in order to gain acceptance.

_____

_____

_____

_____

_____

2. What part of yourself did you change or hide in order to fit in?

_____

_____

_____

3. What did you notice or sense about the situation that compelled you to change something about yourself?

....

....

....

4. Was what you hid or changed about yourself worth it?

....

....

....

5. How will the information in this chapter impact the culture of your classroom?

....

....

....

CHAPTER TWO

RADIOACTIVE RHETORIC

RADIOACTIVE RHETORIC

We live in an era in which it's potentially social suicide to challenge, question, or offer perspectives to any claim or statement that contain any of the following terms:

- Systemic Racism
- White Supremacy
- Implicit Bias
- Microaggressions
- Equity
- White Fragility
- Cultural Appropriation
- Culturally Relevant Teaching
- Anti-Racism

These terms have become radioactive in our society. They are not to be touched for the consequences are dire. You'll be dragged to the center of the town and placed in a stockade, on display for public ridicule until you relent, apologize, or disappear.

> FEAR OF DEATH IS ONLY BE RIVALED BY SOCIAL DISAPPROVAL.
> THE LATTER COULD BE STRONGER.
> —ZUBY, RAPPER, AUTHOR, CREATIVE ENTREPRENEUR

I believe these terms are so radioactive that most educators, while well-intentioned, follow this avoidance rule blindly, subconsciously shutting off that place in their mind that might question, have a question, or need some clarity around these issues.

As a result, much of what gets identified as a problem—or the problem itself—is simply accepted without challenge, context, and/or question. No one wants to endure social disapproval. This is part of our nature as humans. We're tribal. We go along to get along, and with the advent of social media, where everyone has a microphone and a platform, the price of social disapproval is at its highest point in human history. The issues themselves aren't rhetorical; they're real. The fact that we're afraid to challenge the thinking of anyone speaking to these issues causes them to devolve into rhetoric and dogma.

I'm not challenging the existence of the issues. What I am challenging is how bloviating about the *global* issues of inequity has provided cover for the *granular* issues of inequity thriving in your classroom, in your practice, and at your school. Social media is overrun by people shouting out all that's wrong while doing nothing, creating nothing, and risking nothing. Real differences are made by addressing issues and taking action. I knew it was time to speak up! A focus on these global issues to the exclusion of an examination of your school's local issues fall under the headings I call *Selequity* and *Cosmequity*.

SELEQUITY (SELECTIVE EQUITY)

Selequity occurs when a school/district chooses to address inequity on a global level while not addressing the inequitable structures, policies, and practices that exist on their campus.

Selequity

Guiding Question: At your school, is there a gap between issues being addressed and issues that *should* be addressed?

COSMEQUITY (COSMETIC EQUITY)

Cosmequity is Selequity's first cousin. A school or district is engaged in Cosmequity when equity is addressed through cosmetic gestures, to the exclusion of examining and changing local policies, practices, and protocols. Cosmequity creates the optical illusion of equity. For example:

Addressing historical African-American figures other than Dr. Martin Luther King Jr. and Rosa Parks is a nice gesture. But the gesture alone isn't equity, and as a result, it rings hollow as equitable practice.

Many schools have created a diversity library with shelves full of books featuring authors of color and characters of color. The gesture alone is fine, but it, in isolation, is not equity.

When either of these initiatives is done inside a culture of inclusion and belonging combined with a school-wide commitment to equitable instructional practices, then they can be powerful. Cosmequity's deception lies in all the validation the optics produce. It can leave you believing that you're really addressing equity. But, now that you're reading this book, you understand that a new diversity library alone isn't going to move the needle of improved student learning. The optics of diversity aren't enough.

DISMANTLING WHITE SUPREMACY

Many schools and districts are engaging educators in a variety of book studies, webinars, workshops about equity, racism, social justice, bias, and other challenges that result in the identification of negative forces at work outside the schoolhouse. Ruthless Equity places you in front of the mirror, staring at your best opportunity for improvement. As you stare into the mirror, consider these questions:

- Can you be an antiracist and have students being taught below grade-level all year long?
- Is White supremacy responsible for the continued practice of ability grouping at your school?
- At your school, is the most fun, innovative, rigorous, challenging, and engaging instruction reserved for an exclusive subset of your students you've identified as *gifted*? Has this been identified as an equity issue?
- Do you understand that creating intervention groups based on data from standardized test results and not real-time common formative assessment data is both a social justice issue and an equity issue?
- Does your school have several lower-level courses students are tracked into that prevent them from access to grade-level or better instruction?
- Is there a primary emphasis on ranking, sorting, and selecting students?
- Are students at your school who require extra time and support *bathed in their weaknesses* while those regarded as proficient or better are *bathed in their strengths?*

In addition to the questions, consider policies and practices commonly found in schools today:

- You *pobrecito* your Spanish-speaking students, setting them up to be *illiterate* in two languages.

- You *bless your heart* poor White and Black students into a lifetime of learned helplessness and entitlement.
- You have two very active boys in your class. Ritalin is recommended for *DeShawn*, while *Hunter* is regarded as just rambunctious.
- Why do you have systemic gatekeeping for higher-level courses?
- Why you expect less by disruptive behaviors because you don't expect any better from *these* kids.

You get where I'm going with this? Every school has some form of this going on today—issues in the form of policies, practices, or protocols that can be examined *today* and changed *today* in the service of providing equity for each and every student we serve. But instead of sweeping our own porch, we look out the window and become a member of The Pontification City Choir and help sing their hits songs that are often about "systemic this" and "institutional that." And just like that, you go from identifying changes *you* can make, to focusing on changes *they* need to make. Who is *they* you ask?

Well, *They,* is the Boogeyman.

Stop chasing The Boogeyman.

GET GRANULAR, NOT GLOBAL.

TAKE THE HELIUM OUT OF EQUITY

What should concern every educator is how equity has become more about politics than practice. It's been twisted into an issue to discuss, and not act upon. Equity has been twisted into feelings and theories, and not practice. Some circles associate equity solely with race and culture. Equity has become all confrontation and no aspiration. Equity in other circles is addressing issues for a better future, a brighter tomorrow, and avoiding issues that impact students you serve tomorrow; as in Wednesday if you're reading this on Tuesday. With so much noise, and so little clarity, defining equity has been left to the user in any given moment, to fit their prevailing agenda or narrative.

Equity is being fractured in schools and spread it so thin that it's becoming difficult to grasp. Equity has moved from the measurable, actionable, practical, and impactful to that of dogma and rhetoric. This causes equity to float up into the ether like a balloon filled with helium. Once an issue moves from tangible to theoretical, we go from action and results to inaction and rhetoric.

It should surprise no one that education is now overrun by reactionary race-baiters, equity hucksters, and for-profit-policy pimps who play on your fears and honest concerns, to distract you from the real work that needs to be done. These opportunists have polluted our profession, capitalizing on the anger and frustration of marginalized groups, and at the same time, leveraging historical guilt, shame, and blame of White educators. The common thread in their approach with both groups is shining a light and exposing real issues of inequity, racism, low expectations, bias, elitism, and other important issues, without providing practical solutions and an aspirational vision.

The best course of action to address *systematic this* or *institutional that* is to address the issues in the context of equitable practice. In other words, leveraging equitable instructional practices rooted in a culture of inclusion and belonging is the fertile soil from which issues are best addressed. Concerns around equity will grow from the soil of practice, not preaching.

FOR THE WHITE AND WOKE

It takes courage to call out policies that have as their underpinnings elements of racism, bias, or White supremacy. Confronting inequity in any form doesn't absolve you of the responsibility to ensure equity for the students you serve. In the summer of 2021, I was the keynote speaker at a principals conference in Colorado. Leadership and equity were major themes of the event. In addition to the keynote, I also participated as a member of a four person panel. The three other panelists were current K-12 principals serving schools in Colorado.

The most vocal panelist was an elementary school principal who happened to be a White woman. She leads a poor-performing elementary school serving a community primarily made up of students of color from families living in poverty. Her first opportunity to address the audience was a bold declaration calling for a dismantling of White supremacist influences on state learning standards.

She made a connection between the impact of White supremacy on elements of the state standards and assessments. She made a direct connection between her students' poor performance and the state learning standards. She repeatedly cited White supremacist influences as a reason the standards had no regard for cultural responsiveness and as a result, set her students up for failure. This information provides the context for what this principal says next, upon which I invite you to reflect. She goes on to describe how White supremacist influences on Colorado learning standards have impacted achievement at her school:

"Our standardized test data are trash. We have trash data. Our kids are more than a test score, and we focus on knowing them relationally." They choose to focus on relationships and knowing something about every student, placing a large emphasis on social-emotional learning, or SEL (which most often means while the **S**ocial and **E**motional aspects of SEL are being addressed, we'll take a break from **L**earning).

My interpretation of her conclusion is this: As a result of "existing White supremacist structures in our system," our students cannot succeed, and the proof is in our (trash) data. My decoding of her conclusion: It's the Boogeyman's fault, and it's our job to call it out, not fix it.

This was one of the most damaging examples of Selequity I've ever experienced. The White supremacy-laden curriculum is the cause of the massive failure at our school, and as a result, we have a different standard of learning for our students. This scenario is dangerous because students, staff, and leadership are lulled to sleep under the warm blanket of another woke cause heroically standing front and center, with no solutions in sight.

This was an awkward crossroad moment. I was shocked and trying to process what I just heard while trying to decide if and how to respond. I could feel time running out. At the last second before the moderator moved the discussion forward, I spoke up. With as much professionalism and empathy as I could muster, this is the gist of my response that day: "Well, I can appreciate where your heart is, but I've got news for you. The world will not judge your students differently. The trail of failure will follow those students, and their data will not contain an asterisk denoting special circumstances. There won't be a note attached to their academic records that reads, "these students failed because of White Supremacist structures in our curriculum." No, they'll be looked upon as failures while you and I continue to live our upwardly mobile lives, earning promotions, and attending events like this one."

THERE IS A FINE LINE BETWEEN THEY SHOULDN'T HAVE TO LEARN THIS, AND THEY CAN'T LEARN THIS.

Both sides of the above statement concern me. *They shouldn't have to learn this* is the call of the *woke* and *They can't learn this* is the call of the racist. The goal of the woke is to support. The goal of the racist is to suppress. However, there's a stink on both of these goals. They are two sides of the same coin. There are opposite intentions that often lead to the same results; low expectations, low efficacy, and poor results. The negatives of the *can't learn* part of the statement is obvious. The *shouldn't learn* part of the statement is less obvious. Let's break it down a little further.

When specific learning standards, skills, and outcomes have been identified as ones that *some students* shouldn't have to master due to issues of bias, access, lack of cultural responsiveness, or any other reason, aspersions aren't cast upon the standards themselves, aspersions are cast upon the segment of that student population. Even when the standard is seen as inappropriate, it doesn't negate that segment of the student population from being looked upon as broken. Even when all of the research lines up, the societal reality is interpreted as, *These* students can't learn like *other* students. I hear passionate learning standards arguments made on behalf of Black and Latino students, but where's the same outcry for Asian students? I don't see protests about learning standards Asian students shouldn't be expected to learn. If you've seen protests about what Asian students shouldn't have to learn, let me know. I'll wait.

The principal's heart was in the right place. What she didn't realize is that her excuses absolved her from owning the current reality of her students. She and her staff don't have to own the results, the solutions, or the work. The decision they made was to focus on relationship building. Relationship building that isn't in the direct service of ensuring high levels of learning for every student is a dressed-up, woke version of low expectations. There are devastating ripple effects students will suffer as result of this dance with Selequity:

- You allow students to regard themselves as victims, which will likely inform their life choices for decades.
- You cast students as broken and unable to learn like other students.
- Expectations of students calibrate down.
- You render yourself powerless to effect change.
- You devolve into doing charity work, "you're doing a favor" for *these* poor kids with pity and kindness and empty relationship building.

Others might be fooled by the accolades received from this form of virtue signaling, but now you know better, and your Grumpy Uncle knows better.

You don't get to use student failure as evidence of the existence of White supremacy.

Ensure When Things Are Unfair

Guiding Question: How will this approach and mindset impact your practice?

I write this full of piss and vinegar because it makes me think about three educators with whom I've worked, and how they respond to challenges their students bring to table. The three leaders I highlight support schools that cover a wide spectrum of challenges often offered up as excuses for why students can't learn at high levels; urban schools, rural schools, schools with a history of underperformance, poverty, transient community, students with a first language other than English, Title I, among others. They acknowledge inherent inequities in teaching, learning, and assessment systems. And yet, they do not see the issue as excusing them from pursuing equity for every student. They advocate for needed change, but don't stand pat waiting for the change to take place. They continue to leverage the collective genius of teachers in the service of every student performing at standard or better. They are ruthless. All three of these leaders have Ruthless Equity DNA. I'm going to highlight specific aspects of their leadership and practice that are aligned with ensuring learning for every student.

Paula Maeker

Paula Maeker is a former school leader and a current instructional coach and school consultant. I worked with Paula while she served at Zwink ES and Canyon Springs ES in the greater Houston area. Hands down, she is one of the most competitive educators I know; but not in the way you might think. She doesn't compete to be seen as the best, she doesn't compete against other teachers, she competes with marginalizing labels and fixed mindsets. Paula is a woman of class and grace, that is, until she overhears you talking about what kids can't do, can't learn, and can't achieve. Because that's the moment when the earrings come off and the Vaseline comes out. She's ready to fight, and her choice of weapons are sound practice, collaboration, influence, creativity, urgency, innovation, relentless learning, and indomitable will.

I've encountered many educators who claim to love working with *those kids,* but most of them focus more on cultivating relationships, and don't prioritize grade-level or better achievement. For Paula, every student growing to grade-level or better achievement is the only lens she knows, and developing meaningful relationships with students aids her in that mission. Paula Maeker is ruthless about high-levels of learning for every student.

Dr. Anisa Baker-Busby

Dr. Anisa Baker-Busby is a current school principal and she consults with schools nationally. She leads a school in rural Georgia that has many of the challenging trappings of schools in urban areas. Lindsey Elementary has a buffet of freshly baked excuses for why they should be underachieving. But, Dr. Baker-B will have none of it. Like a great classroom teacher, Anisa speaks greatness into the *students* in her *classroom;* her staff. In the face of challenge after challenge, she understands her role as chief hunter/gatherer.

She hunts for everything her staff needs to do the right work. She gathers the PD, tools, supports, and time for teachers to ensure high levels of learning for all students. She goes further than "no excuses." Dr. Baker-Busby leads a culture of "no excuses with support."

She understands that her investment capacity building is the key to student improvement. She leverages the collective expertise of staff. Anisa is a warm demander, and willing to have the hard conversation. And since seeing results improve, her staff runs through walls for their students. Dr. Anisa Baker-Busby is ruthless about teacher efficacy and empowerment. She hunts and gathers everything they need to make equity happen for every student.

Brig Leane

Brig Leane is a current instructional coach and school consultant. He's a former school leader at Fruita Middle School in Fruita, Colorado. When you meet Brig, you'll want him to be your friend. After meeting him, my dad would turn to me and say, he's *good people*. He's one of the nicest people I know. Fruita MS was in the throes of underperformance. There was no shortage of effort, but student learning results lagged. They were frustrated, and looking around for answers. They not only wanted to improve student learning results, but were somewhat lost trying to figure out how to make it happen.

After speaking with Brig and the members of their leadership team about:

- the power of being mission-driven
- the power of shared vision
- aligning every decision with shared mission and vision
- clarity of support around school-wide collective commitments
- The proverbial "light came on" and Team Fruita were off and running.

Brig and his team got clear about their priorities and used their shared mission at their North Star. They worked to establish clarity around essential outcomes in every course and content area. The clarity around what teams had to ensure every student mastered fostered increased collaboration, and as results improved, staff confidence improved as well. Clarity didn't stop with staff. Students carried a card with specific course essential learning outcomes listed. Every time they demonstrated mastery of an essential outcome, they received a stamp, which eventually led to rewards offered by businesses in the community. The momentum created led to Fruita's transformation.

Fruita Middle School went from a school of *independence* to *interdependence*. They moved from the lowest organizational health index in their twenty-two thousand student school district to the highest over five years. Brig Leane is ruthless about improving results through clarity and alignment.

While their styles are different, their mission isn't. They are ruthless about ensuring high levels of learning for all students, regardless of background. They'd turn to their equity warriors and declare their commitment to hunt and gather whatever their staffs needed to get the right work done. They'd move hell and high water to provide whatever it took to ensure learning. For them, there are no excuses, even when there *are* excuses.

By the way, two of the three leaders I highlighted happen to be White. This isn't a statement about White educators, I mention it to emphasize that excellence in leadership has universal competencies that transcend race and culture. I also notice patterns, I do the math, and then I speak on it. Unfair conditions must be dismantled, and until they are, we must work to ensure equity for all students, even in the midst of unfair circumstances. There's no helium in the equity efforts of these leaders. They lean into clarity and school-wide collective commitments aligned with equity for all.

RUTHLESS REMINDERS

- The more ambiguous we are, the less accountable we have to be.
- The most effective way to "dismantle" the world's "institutional/systemic" social issues is to start by dismantling them in your practice, on your team, and at your school.
- You'll get empty praise and credit for gestures of Selequity and Cosmequity from many who don't know any better. But you now know better. Neither, in isolation, moves the needle for student learning. Neither, in isolation, is equity.
- Your commitment to dismantle any form of inequity isn't an invitation to accept students' failure. Do not use student failure as data for your cause. This is just another form of charitable pandering doused with the cologne of advocacy.

DISRUPTIVE ACTION TO TAKE

With a team of colleagues, discuss the following questions:

What changes have been made in your practice/mindset in the service of equity?

What examples of Selequity and Cosmequity have you seen on your campus?

What inequitable practices need to be dismantled in your class-room and at your school?

CHAPTER THREE
COMPLACENCY: THE ENEMY OF EQUITY

IDENTIFYING THE ENEMY IS A HUGE FIRST STEP, BUT NOT THE ONLY STEP. IT'S IMPORTANT TO DISSECT THE ENEMY SO WE CAN SEE WHAT SHE FEEDS ON.
—TAYLOR HARPER, LEAD LEARNER, INNOVATIONS

THERE IS AN ENEMY

There is an enemy.

The enemy is skilled at creating doubt.

The enemy is focused on creating distraction and division.

The enemy is cunning and seductive.

The enemy is relentless.

The enemy is out to destroy your confidence.

The enemy wants you to feel helpless.

The enemy wants you to pity more than you persist.

The enemy will try and convince you that Black, Latino, and poor White students cannot learn at mastery levels.

That equity for all isn't possible.

And the hardest part to swallow is...

The enemy is **YOU**.

THE UNTAPPED TEACHER WITHIN

Most of us embody two educators. The educator we are and the educator we've always dreamed of being. Between the two educators stands Complacency.

Have you ever:

- attended a conference and learned about new practices you intend to act on, only to return to school where you end up implementing none of them?

- had an idea you didn't share for fear of what a colleague or teammate might think?

- stayed quiet when you know you should've advocated for a student, a teammate?

- decided not to try something creative due to fear that you'd be seen as showing off?

- found yourself leaning more into student factors you don't control and leaning away from your own talent, skills, creativity, and innovation?

- failed to speak your mind, share new ideas, or offer an alternative way of thinking?

- tossed aside new practices because of an uncomfortable learning curve?

- allowed labels to lower your expectations for students?

If so, then you've stood face to face with several forms of a force determined to keep you from being the best version of yourself; and that force is **Complacency**.

Complacency defined: Contentment to a fault with oneself or one's actions.

Definitions of Complacency often highlight someone becoming content. It implies a willful "falling short" of goal and purpose. I'm taking creative license with this definition because teachers don't begin their careers thinking, *I can't wait to fail kids today.*

The word Complacency connotes a sense of ease and contentment with the status-quo. It's a rare thing to hear the word Complacency used in a positive way; there's always a sense of scolding to it. Complacency is far more than a condition or a state of mind. In the world of education, Complacency is an immutable force of nature.

Complacency aligns itself against the educator in seductive, manipulative, and relentless ways. This book isn't meant to scold but to create an awareness of what Complacency does to educators. Teaching is a calling, one of the noblest professions in our society. It's the profession that creates all others. As powerful as the calling to teach is, there is a diametric force at play, and it has proven to be as powerful. Complacency is that force, and its strength is in its numbing effect.

During times when it's calm and quiet, do you find yourself fearful of letting your guard down because you'd see the educator you once aspired to be, were born to be, want to be? If so, you know what Complacency is. Complacency is the most corrosive force in education. It is the root of more educator unhappiness, underperformance, and low expectations. It destroys educator confidence and separates the educator from his gifts. Complacency shrouds your soul. It tamps you down and makes you less than your best.

You must declare Complacency the enemy for it prevents you from the infinite possibilities that lie within. Complacency is capitalized in this book so as to both emphasize it and demonize it. Can you begin to see why you must be ruthless in your pursuit of equity for each of your students?

Complacency is stronger than steel, as fluid as water, more deceptive than an international spy, and more seductive than any classic-Hollywood movie vamp. We've all had our butts kicked by Complacency so know that you're not alone. Sometimes you don't even realize you're on the canvas, KO'd by Complacency, being counted out by the referee. It's time to stiffen your back and stand up to Complacency. Stop taking credit for improved student learning results while pointing away from yourself when results decline. Since you're already working hard, let's make improved student learning a predictable experience! Predictions will no longer be based on the students you receive but on the transformational habits of mind and practice you to which you commit.

It's time for educators to stop casting themselves as victims and martyrs. No strength can be derived from those mindsets. It's time to show the world why education is the profession that creates all professions. And this must be communicated with results, not rhetoric.

Take a look inside your soul because unless I'm insane, or you're dead, there is a voice, barely audible and struggling to be heard. The voice is telling you to take charge, take control, and be the change you want to see in the students in your charge and the teammates with whom you collaborate. Do you feel that voice gaining strength? It's telling you to stop wondering if you can *make* a difference and instead know you *are* the difference!

What I also know is Complacency, taking the form of a gremlin, just climbed up your right arm and is now standing on your shoulder. While I'm delivering coaching through your left ear, Complacency is in your right ear, trumpeting diametrically opposed messages. Don't listen to that familiar voice of fear and doubt and regress to the status-quo.

COMPLACENCY SEEKS TO SABOTAGE

Since Complacency is internal, the very nature of Complacency is self-sabotage. Getting out of our own way so we can focus on the right work is enough of a daily challenge. But there's another form of Complacency you must guard yourself against:

Sabotage from Others

When you do battle with Complacency, you may find colleagues acting strangely. Your team has hit a wall with students who require more time and support to master essential learning outcomes. You believe you've tried everything, and in the eleventh hour, you come up with a new idea. When you share the idea, it's met with cool energy from teammates. Complacency is showing itself in the form of your teammates' energy and affect. When you summon the courage to overcome Complacency, you can become a mirror for fearful and less-secure colleagues.

They see your new idea as a threat as it places their own battles with Complacency front and center. You sense a vibe of, "*Who do you think you are? We weren't successful in meeting the needs of these students, so why do you believe you can be successful?*"

You may also encounter:

- reactions of cynicism and sarcasm toward your efforts
- sarcastic comments delivered in a lighthearted fashion
- accusations of trying to show teammates up
- teasing about you trying to become the "principal's pet"

Comments from colleagues who are closer to the educators' orbit can hit you on a more visceral level. What you don't realize is, they are trying to sabotage you. Complacency sometimes shows up when a teammate grapples with unhealthy levels of perfectionism. Perfectionism that makes the idea you offered a manifestation of colleagues' own perceived failures.

Have you heard the saying, "crabs in a barrel?" Legend has it that crabs will pull down any crab that attempts to climb out of the barrel that holds them in. Your efforts to improve and embed equity result in teammates feeling jealous, threatened, or filled with a sense of self-loathing. These feelings can result in them pulling you back down into the barrel.

LEARNING IS THE THROUGH-LINE OF OUR WORK

One of the blessings that arose from cultural change that began around 2020 is the long-overdue attention given to issues of equity and social justice. One of the challenges accompanying this blessing is the sheer complexity of the topics. When you expand the issues to those of racism, bias, inequity, and other problems, the number of legitimate issues increases exponentially, leaving many educators in various states of confusion, frenzy, and even numbness. I was not immune to this sudden tidal wave of issues.

I reflected on how I could support educators manage the many directions these issues can go. After a period of stillness, it became clear to me. Amid the noise and the smoke and the fog, I concentrated on finding my personal *why* within in the fray. I looked upward to locate My Why, My North Star, and there she was, like a beacon in the fog:

> My Why is coaching schools to leverage the collective expertise of educators and deliver on the promise of **equity, excellence,** and **achievement** for **ALL** students, regardless of background.

The frenzy of current events and issues around equity, racism, and social justice tore me away from my Why temporarily. It had me questioning my messaging and my purpose. Finding my Why and tethering myself to it helped me develop a filter. There's no way any one person can address every important issue surrounding equity and social justice. But early on, I felt pressure to attempt to do just that. Once I quieted the noise, my purpose came clear to me: to address equity and social justice in the context of what directly impacts learning for every student.

In English, that means I focus on the components of equity that move the needle of achievement, that ensure high-levels of learning for all students, and that set educators up to be their best, with opportunities to get even better. What came clear to me is:

LEARNING IS THE THROUGH-LINE OF OUR WORK.

I drive two vintage cars: a 1972 Buick Riviera and a 1975 Oldsmobile Delta-88 Royale convertible. Driving them *is* my meditation. And as a result, I look for opportunities to *run errands for no reason.* They are not show cars that have been restored to mint condition and driven twice a year. My cars are daily drivers, and weather permitting, I drive one or both on almost a daily basis. That's an accomplishment considering that both cars are *stock,* which means neither has been restored and each has its original engine and many original parts.

I've learned a lot about minor repairs and improvements, and for the issues I can't and don't tackle, I trust the cars' care to the team at Litz Automotive, a repair shop about ten minutes from my home. At Litz, auto repair and maintenance that keeps vehicles drivable is the through-line of their work. Vehicle repair and maintenance is their *fundamental purpose.* It's what they do. Everything they do is a direct response to the evidence provided by one of two types of factors:

- What factors *advance* the drivability of the vehicles they service?
- What factors *impede* the drivability of the vehicles they service?

Therefore, every policy, purchase, training procedure, and practice is aligned with their fundamental purpose. The team at Litz provides great customer service. They are attentive, relational, well-informed, and honest. They know many of their clients by name, and go out of their way to make you feel comfortable. They aren't relational just for the sake of being relational. They're relational because it advances their *fundamental purpose*: repairing and maintaining vehicles.

Regarding our profession, the approach to equity and social justice should be no different. As obvious as this sounds, I've seen many well-intentioned educators get pulled away from our fundamental purpose: *ensuring student learning.* This is Complacency at work. Complacency creates distractions and diversions that can cause educators to separate the guiding principle from their work. I hear things like:

- Students are more than test scores.
- We should build relationships *before* we teach.
- We should address SEL (social-emotional learning) *before* instruction.
- There are more important issues than instruction.

I disagree with all these notions. I don't take issue with the spirit of these ideas, just the execution. There should be no "separating out" learning to achieve these outcomes. The above items are important and should be addressed in the *context* of learning, not *instead* of learning. Every issue we address should be in the context of its impact on learning. Therefore, *learning* never stops.

ADVANCE OR IMPEDE—THAT'S ALL

We must treat learning in schools with the same approach. Everything we do must be in the context of whether it *advances* or *impedes* learning. Everything we do is to advance learning. Everything we *start* doing, *continue* doing, or *stop* doing should be in direct response to its impact on learning. This means we do more of what advances learning and intervene with issues that impede learning. We never stop the car (learning). We may slow the car down to address objects in the road that might impede our ability to drive, but we don't stop the car.

Paula Maeker, one of the leaders I highlighted earlier, guides teams through one of the most effective applications of this principle. It would be short-sighted and out of touch to suggest that teachers should just barrel through challenging circumstances brought on by events like the pandemic. While I don't subscribe to *learning loss* as an excuse for why students aren't learning, I do acknowledge that circumstances brought on by the pandemic created drastic change in the learning setting, halted learning for some, and forced educators to embrace a *less is more* paradigm.

In coaching collaborative teams, Maeker finds the sweet spot. She balances empathizing with teachers over the stress caused by lost instructional time and keeping the learning car moving forward. She calls her approach, *half and hone.* In this post-pandemic world, the notion of teachers covering as much content now, as they did prior to the pandemic is impossible, and suggesting otherwise is the blueprint for teachers burning out. Paula coaches teams through a protocol where first, they review the essential outcomes expected for a school year (prior to the pandemic); next, they work together and identify the *most essential* half of the list, and start with them. Her thinking is, *some* essential outcomes mastered is better than *no* essential outcomes mastered. Teachers focus on students mastering the first half of essential learning outcomes, and with any remaining time, chip away at the second half. So, they didn't reduce the number of essential learning outcomes. The mere dividing in half allowed teachers made the work viable during such a chaotic time. A space was created for teachers organize, prioritize, and eat the learning elephant one bite at a time.

COMPLACENCY IS OUR DARK PASSENGER

Even while walking in the dark, each one of us casts a shadow. This shadow is our dark passenger, and the dark passenger of the educator is Complacency. As powerful as our soul's call is to ensure equity, there is a force of nature aligned against that mission, a cunning master of disguise, euphemisms, distractions, and manipulation. It is self-created, self-generated, and self-perpetuated. Complacency is the enemy within.

As educators, there are times when Complacency has gotten the best of each of us. So often, we succumb to the slow numbing that happens when Complacency invades. That bastard has knocked me on my behind too. In my work, I've encountered educators pummeled by Complacency, sadly unaware of how and why. As a reminder, Complacency takes many different forms. I want you to be aware and recognize them. You'll know Complacency has entered the room with your favorite latte in hand when you:

- lower your expectations because circumstances broke your heart
- create another "low group" in your classroom
- dial back the rigor of a task because "these kids" aren't ready
- lower your expectations upon learning that a student has an IEP
- expect less of students from *that* neighborhood
- abandon a new practice after a few "unsuccessful" tries and decide it won't work with *this population*
- fail to contact parents with concerns because they're not as involved as they should be

Have there been times when you get a flash in your mind's eye of you at your best? You see yourself operating with the confidence that if you don't have the answer, you'll find it? And then in the next moment, become consumed with doubt, and you dismiss the vision as unrealistic? If so,

You know what Complacency is.

Are you a leader who isn't leading? An innovator who isn't innovating? A connector who isn't connecting? A trailblazer who isn't blazing? An out-of-the-box thinker stuck inside the box? A status-quo disruptor who isn't disrupting? If so, then

You know what Complacency is.

In his book *Overcoming the Achievement Gap Trap*, Dr. Anthony Muhammad issues a wake-up call: "People tend to ignore change that is potentially inconvenient and challenging in exchange for dogma and rhetoric that make them feel better. A dilemma exists in our society as it relates to educational equality and the difficult changes that it requires. It resonates with our souls conceptually, but I question the collective will to endure the discomfort necessary to make it a reality." This is Complacency at work.

Learning Loss Mandate

Guiding Question: How much power have you given the notion of "learning loss?" How has "learning loss" altered your expectations for student learning?

COMPLACENCY IS INVISIBLE

Complacency cannot be seen. It's odorless, tasteless, and takes no physical form. However, its impact can be felt. It can take the form of data that makes you second-guess your expectations. Imagine a second-grade team analyzing data from a common formative assessment. The protocol for this process directs the team to:

1. Provide extension and enrichment opportunities for students who've demonstrated mastery of learning outcomes.
2. Identify students who require more time and support to master essential learning outcomes.
3. Regroup students identified in step two by specific learning needs.
4. Share individual teaching strategies to determine if one strategy proved more effective than the others.

The protocol focuses the team on supporting students by *name* and by *need*. Here's where Complacency slides in. The dialogue veers off the protocol when teammates begin citing outside factors as reasons why their students aren't mastering the content.

Factors such as:

- well, you know they're *low*
- our *demographic* is changing.
- *these* kids don't get support at home.
- Aren't we expecting too much from *them*?

As a result, the team abandons the protocol and now has excuses not to improve their practice. Students lose because educators don't grow and get better. Teachers lose because they miss opportunities to grow and get better. In this scenario, Complacency took a corrosive approach to the destruction of educator efficacy. It persists and wears you down over time. It is death by a thousand small cuts, small retreats, small doubts, and small compromises.

READER, COMPLACENCY CAN BE BEATEN

Otherwise, our field would never know the likes of Dr. Rick DuFour, Dr. Bob Eaker, Becky DuFour, Marva Collins, Jaime Escalante, Dr. Yvette Jackson, Dr. Anthony Muhammad, Sister Mary Claire (my second-grade teacher), Dr. Lorraine Monroe, Mike Mattos, Dr. Gloria Wade-Gayles, and many others. However, to defeat Complacency, we have to make a commitment to show up differently. Because when Complacency shows up, it is already in mid-season form, baby. Complacency is on its A-game from the moment the contest starts, and it's out to win by any means necessary.

Complacency has its own playbook. It knows how we play offense and how we play defense. Complacency knows our patterns and tendencies. We need to change our plays, alter our mindset, and change our patterns. What does "showing up differently" look like? Next up: Ruthless Equity.

RUTHLESS REMINDERS

- Complacency stands between the educator we are and the one we've always dreamed of being.

- Complacency aligns itself against the educator in seductive, manipulative, and relentless ways.

- Learn to recognize Complacency in the form of sabotage by others.

- Ensuring learning is our fundamental purpose and the through-line of our work.

DISRUPTIVE ACTION TO TAKE

With a team of colleagues, discuss the following questions:

Within this chapter, which ideas stand out?

_____

_____

_____

How are you reacting to this information?

_____

_____

_____

What do you commit to do differently as a result of your reflection?

_____

_____

_____

CHAPTER FOUR
RUTHLESS EQUITY

EQUITY EXPLAINED THROUGH IMAGERY

In the context of our work, it's important for me to knock the theory, rhetoric, and ambiguity out of equity. I'm going to use an adaptation of very popular illustrations explaining the difference between *equality* and *equity,* and connect it to our work. Let's assume the people in the images are students. Let's also decide that what we want them to achieve is "essential." Here's the question:

In this image, what is the essential outcome we *must ensure* for each student?

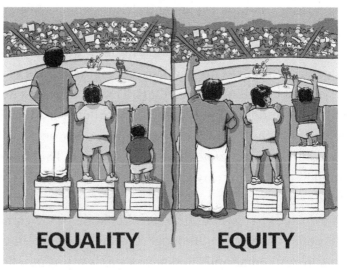

EQUALITY   EQUITY

Interaction Institute for Social Change | Artist: Angus Maguire

The answer: We must ensure each student can see the game from an unobstructed view.

When you look at the equality side of the image, each student is provided with the same support. However, on the equity side of the image, each student has been provided *what they need, when they need it, with urgency (no delay)* to achieve this essential outcome. There is a critical element of equity in this image, an essential outcome. Equity requires a culture of belonging and inclusion, *and* the presence of an essential learning outcome.

Equity cannot be achieved without an essential outcome. There are no exceptions. This is as fundamental as you trying to explain wetness without water, or breathing without air. The call to action in our equity work is identifying essential learning outcomes in every course and content area.

Ruthless Equity defined: In a culture of belonging and inclusion, organizing to provide each student what s(he) needs when s(he) needs it, with urgency to ensure mastery of essential learning outcomes.

FROM EXCUSES TO CONTEXT

Let's further examine the equality/equity image. We could brainstorm a long list of excuses for these three students and why we can't ensure they watch the game from an unobstructed view. We can generate excuses around lack of resources, lack of home support, ambulatory issues, and others. There will always be excuses to justify why students don't learn. The challenges, adversity and obstacles don't disappear. Ruthless Equity educators aren't detached from reality. What changes is your perspective. The challenges once offered as *excuses* for why students can't learn now become *context* for your response.

Moving adversity from the excuses column to the context column isn't rooted in "positive thinking." The shift is rooted in the word *essential.* Every course and content area has learning outcomes that fall into two general categories, "need to know" learning outcomes and "nice-to-know" learning outcomes. Once you've identified learning outcomes that are essential, it follows logically that you organize to ensure every student masters them. Once you've identified a learning outcome as essential, then these former *excuses* become current *context* for your response:

- who the student is
- where he's from
- where she lives
- what he looks like
- what his reputation is
- where her current level of performance is
- who his mommy is
- who her daddy is
- parents' income
- family reputation or history
- the language he speaks or doesn't speak
- the labels used to define them

Your mission is to build scaffolds to move students from where they are to mastery. This cannot be overstated. The challenges that once created excuses, the *yeah-buts*, and rationalizations about why a student can't learn no longer apply. These challenges now serve to activate your creativity, will, innovation, and urgency. They're to be treated as factors you work around, jump over, slide under, or break through to ensure mastery of essential learning outcomes.

RUTHLESS EQUITY EXPLAINED

The word "ruthless" is rarely used to describe anything positive and almost never to describe anything related to education. Merriam-Webster's Collegiate Dictionary defines ruthless as: having or showing no pity or compassion for others. Ruthless Equity has nothing to do with being ruthless with people. In your pursuit of equity for all, you must be ruthless in two specific areas: factors and excellence.

Factors: Apply ruthless focus to factors aligned with equitable practice, and be equally ruthless about cutting away the factors that impede your ability to execute equitable practice.

Excellence: Reflect on the level of focus, sacrifice and dedication required to become Olympic athletes. What we don't associate this level of excellence with is a commitment to ruthlessness. Olympic athletes are ruthless about where they invest their time and energy. Time is finite so, to be excellent at anything, you can't give your time, talent, and energy to everything.

Excellence requires a ruthless commitment to factors that advance your mission and an equally ruthless exclusion of factors that do not.

THERE IS A RUTHLESSNESS TO EXCELLENCE.

What Equity Is and Isn't

Guiding Question: Is there school-wide clarity around what equity is and isn't?

YOU HAVE BEEN RUTHLESS

Recall a time in your personal life when you had to make something happen in the face of seemingly insurmountable odds. In your mind, failure was not an option, but "the math" of the situation didn't add up. It might not have been a life-or-death situation, just one you deemed important enough to get done. With odds stacked against you, any reasonable person would conclude your chances of success as highly unlikely at best! Yet you ignored that reasonable person and marched on. Imagine that right now, you're facing that obstacle.

You're aware of the odds, the obstacles, the challenges, and the adversity with which you're confronted. But failure isn't an option in your mind. You symbolically place your back against the wall and decide you must get it done!

Your first idea doesn't work. Instead of succumbing to defeat, you move to the next idea with calculated precision. Everything unrelated to accomplishing your mission takes a back seat. People close to you understand this. Those not close to you quickly feel the force of your intensity and get the hell out of your way. You're operating in a state of ruthlessness. And while it isn't any guarantee of success, in the end, you succeed far more than not, when you give yourself over to ruthlessness.

This approach isn't appropriate for every learning outcome. If it was, you'd burn out as an educator. Ruthlessness is reserved for the pursuit of mastery learning of essential standards. You will do battle with Complacency because Ruthless Equity moves "learning for all" from a cliché, to **your mission.**

THE ONLY QUESTION EQUITY ANSWERS

Ensuring equity for every student requires a literal approach to the word "essential." Any learning outcome regarded as essential means we must organize to ensure every student achieves mastery. The questions of *can they learn?* or *can't they learn?* are no longer relevant. This leaves us with the **ONLY** question that matters. The only question the pursuit of equity answers:

HOW WILL <u>WE</u> GET <u>EVERY</u> STUDENT THERE?

Operating with this mindset is an exercise, the building of a critical mindset muscle. Building this mindset muscle will be challenging, especially when you're familiar with the history, performance, and reputation of your students. It's challenging when you bring bias and assumptions about students to your work.

You and your teammates must engage in a mental game and hold one another accountable to address the only question that matters. You commit to leverage your collective expertise, maximize every minute of your contracted duty day to do whatever it takes to ensure mastery of essential outcomes for every student. This is the approach. So, sit with this for a minute and be sure you're ready to embrace it.

The Only Questions Equity Answers

Guiding Question: Are you ready to experience new levels of teacher creativity, engagement and innovation this question inspires?

URGENCY: PART I

In the pursuit of instructional equity, urgency isn't just a mindset, it also involves structure in the form of time parameters. Urgency requires timeframes. For example: An eighth-grade math team identified six essential learning outcomes that students have to master during the nine-week first marking period of the school year. The team mission is to monitor every student's progress toward mastery of the six identified essential outcomes.

There are a variety of ways to embed urgency into this scenario. Two examples are:

1. Break the marking period into three or four-week segments.
2. Decide which essential outcomes will be covered during which segment.

The configuration of the weeks should be driven by how much time you believe is required before students are able to demonstrate mastery of the essential outcomes. The time parameters create the urgency to maximize time, creativity, innovation, and focus. Don't fear time parameters; embrace them. We are at our best when we create finite conditions in the pursuit of important milestones.

FIFTY/FIFTY

Ensuring equity for each student cannot be achieved through mindset *or* practice. It can only be achieved through a commitment to mindset *and* practice. This work is fifty percent *mindset* and fifty percent *execution.* Every teacher can acknowledge the fact that in every curricular area, there are "need to knows" and "nice to knows." For the "need to knows," you flip a mental switch that moves you into a mode in which you organize, plan, collaborate, and execute as if student mastery is the only outcome. Whether you realize it or not, you've leveraged this potent combination of mindset and practice in your personal life.

Mindset and Intent

Guiding Question: Can you see the difference between *ensuring* students learn and offering students *the opportunity* to learn?

URGENCY: PART II

Have you ever encountered a new mother who, in the face of multiple logistical obstacles, decided that she had to make something (*not* life-threatening) happen for her baby? Did you recognize when that mother snapped into "SEAL Team 6 special-ops" mode, and everyone knew to get out of her way? When mothers flip that switch, they go from mother to *mutha*. And when that happens, all those around who seek to live another day clear a path for her.

While our scenario uses mothers as its example, it should trigger a time in your life when:

- the odds were stacked against you
- creating solutions had you operating at your most open-minded, focused, innovative, creative, and collaborative
- you were open-minded regarding solutions
- excuses were available but not taken
- you did whatever was necessary, because...

ONCE YOU DECIDE SOMETHING MUST HAPPEN, YOU RESPOND DIFFERENTLY.

Though these scenarios weren't life threatening, you operated as if they were. I call this state of mind, "first-world urgency."

FIRST-WORLD URGENCY

We are at our creative and innovative best when **we decide** something **must** happen. We problem-solve and create solutions as if lives depend on our success. First-world urgency is manufactured because of our first-world existence.

Despite what you see in the first 20 minutes of any network news program, we live in a very civilized society. You don't leave the grocery store in a full sprint to your car fearing the possibility of being mauled by a pack of wolves. You don't have to risk hunting bison for dinner. You don't live your daily life in constant "flight-or-flight" mode. Yet, that fight or flight part of our DNA still exists, and we summon it when we have to *manufacture* urgency.

> ## WHEN WE'RE BEING EQUITABLE, WE DON'T GIVE UP ON STANDARDS, AND WE DON'T GIVE UP ON KIDS.
> ## -GEORGINA RIVERA, EDUCATOR, 2ND VICE PRESIDENT, NATIONAL COUNCIL OF SUPERVISORS OF MATHEMATICS

THERE IS NO PASSIVE PATH TO EQUITY

You're going to learn why there is no *passive* path to equity, why equity must be taken by force, why you must be ruthless and relentless in the pursuit of equity for all. You'll *empower* instead of *enable*. You'll *advocate* instead of *save*. You'll make students *powerful* instead of *pitiful*. You will see around corners for them, know better for them, and be in the service of them.

You'll need to reset each day to be ruthless for your students. Why, you ask? Because Complacency is an evil force of nature dead-set on applying unrelenting force in the service of maintaining the status-quo. There is no *passive* path to equity because Complacency is a cunning, seductive, and persuasive opposing force ready and waiting to derail everything you do. While learning how to embed and ensure equity, you'll also find out how to dissect the enemy and cut it out of your practice.

THE 4 RULES OF RUTHLESS EQUITY

At the foundation of Ruthless Equity, there are four "rules of ruthless-ness." The next four chapters are devoted to each rule. Here's a brief overview of each one. Buckle up, as we're about to get surgical, baby!

Ruthless Rule 1: A Commitment to Courage Over Comfort
This first rule challenges your **comfort zone:** There is an inherent discomfort when making paradigm shifts. You're going to commit to disruptive shifts in mindset, policy, and practice. It takes courage to embrace belonging and inclusion. Challenging the status-quo is simultaneously the most powerful and least used lever for creating meaningful change. Your road to ensuring equity will be uncomfort-able at times. You'll also make others uncomfortable. There's no way of escaping it, so embrace it. The ruthless become comfortable with discomfort.

Ruthless Rule 2: A Commitment to Dismantling Ability Groups
This second rule will disrupt the status-quo of your school because ability groups and tracking are inequitable practices, period. There is no way around this fact. There are no exceptions to this fact. Ability groups and every other tracking policy and practice must be disman-tled and eradicated. In this chapter, I'll explain why the practice is inequitable and provide you with a viable equitable alternative.

Ruthless Rule 3: A Commitment to Start with the Crown:
This third rule provides the practical application of **equity.** Equitable practices begin with the commitment to ensuring mastery of agreed-upon essential learning outcomes. Once you identify essential outcomes, all of your energy, focus, intention, creativity, and practice are dedicated to growing every student tall enough to wear the crown (essential learning outcomes). Ruthless Equity starts with the crown, not the kid.

Ruthless Rule 4: A Commitment to Momentum Over Mood Rings
This fourth rule leverages the power of **ruthless consistency.** Most improvement initiatives are short-lived because in the beginning, small changes often appear to make no difference. Schools and districts often jump from one initiative to another, rarely allowing time, process, and practice to produce results. This results in educators being cynical and hesitant about implementing new practices with fidelity. Ruthless Equity is a compounding process that requires a commitment to cycles of practice. Old habits will tempt you. Short-term results may discourage you. You must act in the presence of both temptation and early discouragement. The ruthless don't fall prey to the seduction of short-term data and feedback.

RUTHLESS REMINDERS

- Ruthless Equity defined: Inside a culture of belonging and inclusion, organizing to provide each student what s(he) needs when s(he) needs it, with urgency to ensure mastery of essential learning outcomes.
- Ensuring equity is fifty percent mindset and fifty percent execution.
- To ensure equity, you must manufacture urgency.
- Equity requires an essential learning outcome.
- The pursuit of equity answers one question: How will we get every student there?

DISRUPTIVE ACTION TO TAKE

With a team of colleagues, discuss the following questions:

Within this chapter, which ideas stand out?

....

....

....

How are we reacting to this information?

....

....

....

Where do we see evidence of Ruthless Equity, as defined, at our school? What insights and questions are emerging?

....

....

....

CHAPTER FIVE

THE FIRST RULE OF RUTHLESSNESS
A COMMITMENT TO: COURAGE OVER COMFORT

DISRUPTING THE STATUS-QUO IS A COURAGEOUS ACT. THE DISCOMFORT OF DISRUPTION IS WHERE SIGNIFICANCE IS BORN.

WISH IN ONE HAND...

I, along with my two sisters, grew up in a loving household. Our dad, Carl, is a retired NYC police officer. Our mom was an educator. She was also the disciplinarian, and pretty strict. She had high expectations for us, and although at that time no one in our family had graduated college, you'd never know that from the way our mother spoke of the importance of a college education. In our home, education was a priority.

We didn't grow up in abject poverty, but at times, money was tight. While we never lacked for basic needs, there were periods when we lived from "paycheck to almost paycheck" and sometimes had "more month than the money." As a child, I was sometimes in denial of how tight money was. One day I was out shopping with Mom, and I saw it. As I turned the corner, the toy aisle appeared to part like the Red Sea, leaving one toy in its wake; the new G.I. Joe with the Kung-Fu Grip.

I knew better than to ask Mom for it directly. Instead, I did my best

Black Bobby Brady impression, innocently tilting my head at a 45-degree angle, sending my eyes diagonally upward, and like Bobby, placed my index finger on the corner of my mouth and said, "I sure wish I could have this G.I. Joe with the Kung Fu Grip." Without missing a beat, Mom said:

> WISH IN ONE HAND, SH*T IN THE OTHER.
> SEE WHICH ONE GETS FULLER FASTER.
> —SUZANNE WILLIAMS, MOTHER, WIFE, EDUCATOR

And with that, we kept shopping. I didn't understand the meaning of her remark at the time. All I knew is that it meant G.I. Joe wasn't coming home with me that day. Years later, I came to understand what she meant. Wishing for anything was a waste of time. If you want something, figure out how to make it happen. So, what does this heartwarming story have to do with your work? Everything. You see, with Complacency lurking in the shadows, you're not going to wish equity into existence. You'll need to be ruthless with both intention and intensity to make it happen.

HOW LIFE CHANGES WHEN YOU BECOME RUTHLESS

> IT IS COURAGE, COURAGE, COURAGE, THAT RAISES
> THE BLOOD OF LIFE TO CRIMSON SPLENDOR. LIVE BRAVELY
> AND PRESENT A BRAVE FRONT TO ADVERSITY.
> —HORACE

I didn't change after I became ruthless. I didn't look any different, nor did I achieve any sudden enlightenment. I'm the same person I always was, with the same strengths and shortcomings. I am the same person in many ways, though different in a few important ways. Have you ever stayed at a hotel that required you to insert your room key into a slot to access your floor? Hotels do that for safety reasons. They don't want just anyone having access to the rooms on the property. Becoming ruthless will have the same effect on your thinking. The elevator to the penthouse of your mind will be exclusive to those with the correct card-key.

COMPLACENCY AND VICTIMHOOD

We all know people who declare themselves victims. They make an art out of feeling "put upon." What few realize is the victim often does more "putting upon" those around them than actually being "put upon." When Complacency in the form of victimhood descends and takes a seat in meetings, same questions/comments often arise from educators and teams who deal with "those kids" from "that school."

- How can they expect us to teach kids who come from _____?
- How can we possibly do this without _____?
- If we had parents like the ones in _____, we'd be able to make things happen.

The victim act is a form of passive aggression. The victim draws sympathy from others in all the wrong ways. She seeks to absorb energy and attention not by commitment, action, and effort but by the selfish manipulation of others.

The last school I led as principal had a ninety-five percent poverty rate among the student body and was the poorest performing school in the district. We had some educators who saw this as an opportunity to rewrite the narrative of our school. We also had some staff who believed our situation was hopeless. The latter group of educators focused on what resources we lacked and what our students and families lacked. Some of them felt punished because they worked at our school.

Perceptions of our school were negative. In the eyes of many educators in our district, the experienced teachers on our staff were there because they were either washed up or because they fell out of favor with someone in power. Newer teachers were thought to be at our school because well, they were new and needed a job. These perceptions coupled with high rates of student failure were major reasons why for many, working at our school felt like something that *happened to them*, and not a school where they *belonged*.

The victim starts by offering you a "level-one opportunity" to drop what you're doing and come to their rescue. The message isn't direct. You're supposed to pick up on her energy. If you do respond and attempt to empower the victim to work things out for herself, she will respond with a "level-two opportunity." Here she dismisses any suggestions of empowerment and responsibility. You tried to rise above the issue with your empowerment approach. She's now intent on pulling you back down to address her pain. This requires more of your attention. If you continue to fail to see that she's not interested in problem-solving, she'll keep ratcheting things up, with each level more potent than the last. The underlying message is: Come to the rescue or risk me advancing the drama. Refuse, and the victim will go to "level three," threatening to make your life so miserable that you eventually relent. She'll accuse you of not being understanding and compassionate. She'll accuse you of not siding with her. She may go further and dredge up past instances when you didn't listen to her, pounding you with guilt, until you relent. If you've dealt with the wrath of a person living in victimhood, pay attention.

Being a victim isn't a victimless crime. You are corrosive to yourself and those around you. It's a crippling mindset that not only stunts innovation, grit, and creativity but also derails you from doing your work. The victimhood mindset leaves us powerless to grow, learn, or create change. Every one of us has found ourselves in the clutches of this form of Complacency, and every one of us has also experienced times when we avoided victimhood and stood firmly in our power. As challenging as it may be, I urge you to reflect on both sides of this issue. We're at a place in time in which victimhood is encouraged, sensationalized, and rewarded. Personal responsibility and empowerment are boring and don't get "clicks." The drama of victimhood gets attention; the wrong kind of attention.

I found myself navigating through both the victimhood and empowerment mindset during the quarantine of 2020. Onsite professional development is the largest segment of my company, Unfold The Soul. I've built up a pretty good level of demand over 14 years, and in a flash, it was all canceled. I watched my calendar melt away before my eyes. I found myself in somewhat of a catatonic state, unsure of how to navigate tomorrow, much less the future. I had plenty of factors to blame, and for a short time, I felt powerless.

While I pride myself on being an optimist and problem-solver, this period in history was so full of unknowns, that it humbled me. One of the lessons I learned didn't come in the form of an answer, but a reminder that I have to be willing to accept help from another. That working my way through this period might include more than just muscling through it alone. To this end, my wife Nicole helped me see that amid the growing list of issues I could do nothing about, I still had choices. I could be buried beneath the weight of fear, rapid change, and the unknown, or I could be intentional about identifying opportunities inside the chaos.

I decided to make a list of what I "could control" and "could not control." I chose to become a student again and learn more about delivering professional development in a virtual environment. I gained a new appreciation for virtual learning, and as onsite professional development opportunities slowly picked up in mid-2021, I created both onsite and virtual opportunities, which have expanded my availability while creating more balance in my life. I was not a victim.

VICTIMIZED, NOT VICTIMHOOD

These two words are often blended and treated the same, even though they are anything but. "Victimized" describes a condition or circumstances. As Black man in my fifties, I have many stories of being victimized by police for "DWB" (Driving While Black). A 2019 incident found me in a situation where I saw my entire life flash before my eyes. This incident took place in broad daylight, at a small park 15 minutes from my home. On his lunch break, our son locked his keys inside his car. He got a ride back to work, and I agreed to go to the park and arrange for AAA to arrive and unlock his car door. It was a beautiful day, so I drove my 1975 Oldsmobile Delta 88 convertible.

When I arrived, I went to his car and checked the door handles on the off chance that one of them was unlocked. I then returned to my car; again, a 1975 Delta 88 convertible. I don't repeat the make and model of my car to brag. It's to emphasize that I wasn't driving an ideal getaway car. I imagine my trying the car door handles may have alerted someone in the park, and they notified the police. I sat in my car for the next 45 minutes getting some work done on my laptop. I noticed an officer or two in my periphery, but assumed they were there to discourage high school student truancy.

The AAA service provider contacted me. He pulled into the wrong driveway, which was just one driveway over from my location. I offered to drive to him and lead him back to my son's car. I started my car, and as I approached the end of the driveway exit, a long rubber tire strip, designed to puncture tires in the event of an attempted escape was thrown down, two police cars emerged from both sides of the street blocking the driveway. Two other police cars pulled up behind me, and three additional officers emerged from the forest. All of them had their weapons drawn, and two of the firearms were trained on me, just behind each ear. My calm and repeated explanation of why I was there didn't bring fast resolution to the situation. At least it felt like a long time to me. Without going into all of the details, eventually I was cleared, and while shaken like I've never been shaken before, I got to live another day.

That incident left me both devastated and angry. I was *victimized*. As traumatized as I was, I made a conscious choice about *victimhood*. Though I am aware that I'm never too far away from another "situation,"

I refuse to live as a victim. As I stated above, victimization is a circumstance, and victimhood is a mindset. I am aware *and* strategic, and I refuse to live life as if there is a constant target on my back. I refuse to live as if I don't have access to what the world has to offer. Do I acknowledge that some situations are inherently inequitable and unfair? Absolutely! My parents drummed that into my head, in an effort to help me navigate situations and live to see another day. My parents also emphasized that while life had some unfair circumstances, these could never, ever be used as an excuse for why I wasn't working to live my best life.

Ruthless educators don't shy away from the reality of victimization. They're aware of how circumstances can and do negatively impact the lives of some of their students. At the same time, they don't treat students as victims. They don't enable students who might see themselves as victims. They model empowerment and the power of high-expectations, with support! The equity-focused teacher seeks to empower students to *overcome*, work *around*, and work *through* adversity because their circumstances don't exempt them from having to master essential skills and competencies.

When it came to how these issues could impact our lives, my parent's approach was like that of a coach going through the playbook in preparation for a game. For every advantage the opponent has, the coach isn't preparing to forfeit, but how to counteract the opponent's advantage.

I'm not comparing issues of inequity to a coach preparing for a game. I'm comparing the coach's mindset to that of my parents, and how they raised us, and how it influences my work as an educator. They took a "yes, and" approach to adversity. This approach is all I knew growing up, and all I knew as a classroom teacher. As a teacher, once I was clear on what students had to learn, then any and all of their challenges were approached with the "yes and" mindset. For example:

- *Yes*, you don't get much support at home with your homework, *and*, we've got to figure out a way to work around that issue.

- *Yes*, you don't think you're smart, *and* I'm going to challenge you and prove you wrong.
- *Yes*, you've got a history of not performing well in reading *and* we're going to work together to make you a great reader.
- *Yes*, your family is struggling financially, *and* we're going to find resources to support you.
- *Yes*, you're performing below grade-level, *and* that creates urgency to accelerate you so you can get caught up!

The list can go on and on. You can fill in the "yes, and" blanks with any challenges, and my response would be the same, because ensuring mastery of essential learning outcomes is the only option, which makes all circumstances and adversity issues of context, not excuses.

This approach is what prepares students for "real life," not misplaced sympathy, pity, and dumbing down expectations. Life doesn't level down, not even for those who wear the cloak of victimhood.

Shed the Weight of Victimhood

Guiding Question: How have you applied the principles of victimized vs. victimhood in your own life? How have/will you apply it to your work with students?

ALL MEANS ALL DOES NOT MEAN ALL

Before you pass out, hear me out. While "ALL Means ALL" is a charge for you to ensure that *all* students master essential learning outcomes, this approach doesn't apply to *all* learning outcomes. This moves "ALL Means ALL" from a wishful cliché once relegated to only spirit-wear and posters, to a mission-driven collective commitment that is practical and measurable. Ruthless Equity mindset and practice doesn't apply to *all* learning outcomes, just the ones you identify as essential.

COMPLACENCY AND SELF-PITY

Complacency in the form of self-pity is the simultaneous act of completely abrogating responsibility while absorbing the positive benefits of sympathy and advice.

> "If a person or group concludes that a low station in life is someone else's doing, then responsibility for that condition and fixing that condition will lie on others' shoulders. This can create a great sense of psychological relief that encourages a person or organization to disassociate from fixing the problem."
> —Dr. Anthony Muhammad, author, speaker, educational consultant

The very nature of self-pity is rooted in being simultaneously self-absorbed and numb. The person to be pitied is consumed by outside issues and completely numb to the responsibility of growing and producing results. This is Complacency as Self-Pity. If reading about self-pity causes you to make an audible "mmm, hmm" sound every time you think of another colleague for whom this description fits perfectly, my next two questions for you are:

Do you *feed* the self-pity in others?

Do you *enable* their self-pity?

It's challenging enough when students enter our schools with a victim mentality and mindset. Helping them create shifts in their thinking is not easy, but it is doable as we set them up to experience the positive momentum created by stringing together a series of consistent and meaningful learning wins. But when educators see students as victims, and exhibit signs of self-pity about circumstances outside of their control, it's a recipe for disaster. Muhammad also reminds us, "self-pity is the psychological state of an individual in perceived adverse situations who has not accepted the situation and does not have the confidence or competence to cope with it." How can we combat some of our students' feelings of despair and self-pity if we feel helpless to impact learning in the context of their circumstances? Julia Darcy, a fifth-grade teacher at Greene-Hills School in Bristol, CT, found a way to combat this while working through some of her own challenges brought on by the pandemic.

A PANDEMIC PIVOT-IDENTITY WORK

Julia shares details of her journey which began around December 2020 when she found herself in a bit of a teaching rut: "Looking back, it was definitely a form of pandemic fatigue. It was hard for me to feel like I could do my job well because of many factors that were beyond my control. At the time, I was part of the Teacher Leader Fellowship Academy at Sacred Heart University. Part of the mission of the academy is to give teachers a voice and encourage them to take leadership roles within their district. The director, Dr. Betty J. Sternberg, encouraged us to write, and I found myself writing and reflecting on the pandemic and its impact on my teaching. Sharing my experiences with others somehow re-ignited my teaching spark! I knew I needed to pivot and get back into the game, reconnect with my *why*, and get out of this rut I was in. The academy inspired me to focus on solutions and how to adapt in the midst of the pandemic."

"I met with my principal, Scott Gaudet, and asked him about an email he sent staff a few months prior. Back in the fall, he offered support for teachers to engage in a professional book study. I asked if the professional book study was still an option. I explained that I wanted to read *Cultivating Genius* by Dr. Gholdy Muhammad, and that it would be better if I read it with colleagues."

"What surfaced from our discussions was the importance of *identity* and giving students the space to explore and understand themselves. I'm not sure how often students take the time to really sit and think about who they are and all the different factors that make up their identity. We knew we had to be intentional about communicating to students that yes, your life includes circumstances, but you are not defined by your circumstances. This realization helped our teachers as well."

"We created space to ask students:

- How do you see yourself?
- How do you want to see yourself?
- How do others see you?
- How do you want others to see you?
- What are all the puzzle pieces that make up who you are?
- Where are you from?
- Where is your family from?
- What are your likes? Dislikes? Favorite learning style?
- Where do you see yourself in the future?
- What are your family traditions, cherished holidays?

As teachers, we're are really good at using the first week or two of the school year to get to know students and ask a lot of these questions. Our challenge was creating space and structures that allow our students to explore themselves and share their authentic selves with us. As a book study group, we decided that this work had to move beyond the handful of classrooms represented by our book study members. We explored how it would be possible to provide all students with this opportunity. A core group of us created themed Identity Sequence lessons for every month. The themes open the way for both teachers and students to get to know and share more of themselves."

"Feedback over the first few months of using the Identity Sequences made clear that students feel valued, seen, and heard. We knew that with the demands of teaching, there was a better chance of school-wide implementation if the lessons were created and distributed to every classroom. The lessons are designed for kindergarten through grade 8 teachers to incorporate during the first week of every month. At Greene Hills, we already had a block of time called Squad Block, intended for SEL learning targets. Of course, our identity work is aligned with the purpose of this time."

"In addition to its alignment with existing SEL targets, we deliver lessons during the first week of each month because it provides an opportunity to integrate what we learned into our curricular units. When we know more about our students' identity at the beginning of the units, then we can really think about what purposeful and intentional decisions we can make inside the curriculum so that our students see themselves in the learning. Our sequences help us know who is sitting in front of us, from an identity and strengths-based perspective, which helps teachers to move beyond bias and marginalizing labels."

"Identity work is part of equity work. It reminds me of the children's book *The Day You Begin* by Jacqueline Woodson. One of the book's characters is a girl who arrives at a new school. It highlights the moment she finally feels like she belongs there. That moment occurs the day she sees connections with her classmates, her peers, and her teacher. That's what we want for our students. When we're intentional about sharing the parts that make us who we are, then we will all discover opportunities to connect to students and adults in our classroom community, and foster a powerful sense of belonging."

"We're teaching students, not their circumstance. At Greene Hills School, we've prioritized this and provide teachers and students the space to really understand identity and its different components. We also provide the opportunity for students to share this information. We see it as the only way to truly have a culturally responsive environment. "

STUDENTS CAN'T SEE THEMSELVES IN THE LEARNING IF TEACHERS DON'T KNOW WHO THEY ARE.
—JULIA DARCY

COMPLACENCY IS LIKE PENNYWISE

Complacency is like Pennywise, the monster in Stephen King's terrifying novel, *IT*. In the book, Pennywise torments a group of friends. The group comes to realize that Pennywise assumes the appearance of what each person in the group fears most. In the end, they realize that Pennywise didn't have any inherent power; the victims gave the creature its power. Like Pennywise, Complacency has no strength of its own. Every ounce of its power comes from us. We fuel Complacency with our fears, and false fears come in many forms. Master the fear, and you will conquer Complacency.

BEANNACHT/BLESSING

On the day when the weight deadens
on your shoulders and you stumble,
may the clay dance to balance you.
And when your eyes freeze behind
the grey window and the ghost of loss
gets into you, may a flock of colours,
indigo, red, green and azure blue,
come to awaken in you a meadow of delight.
When the canvas frays in the currach of thought
and a stain of ocean blackens beneath you,
may there come across the waters
a path of yellow moonlight to bring you safely home.
May the nourishment of the earth be yours,
may the clarity of light be yours,
may the fluency of the ocean be yours,
may the protection of the ancestors be yours.
And so may a slow wind work these words
of love around you, an invisible cloak to mind your life.

—John O'Donohue, from "Echoes of Memory"

RUTHLESS TEACHERS SPIRAL IN AND OUT QUICKLY

Let's be real, sometimes complaining feels so damn good, doesn't it? You get going on a good rant about some person or situation you're dealing with, and it can pick up real momentum. Then, without a conscious thought, you find yourself attracting more "complaint allies." This is part of being human, and we all do it. Complaining becomes a form of Complacency when it becomes a pattern of identifying problems while making no effort to find a solution.

Complaining is rooted in blaming others. It's a form of externalization that protects you from the psychological pain of responsibility. Complaining lets yourself off the hook, making it impossible to achieve breakthroughs because you've relinquished ownership of the problem. Complaining provides all the benefits of venting with none of the responsibility of problem-solving.

The ruthless teacher isn't immune to complaining. Living authentically requires an awareness of the reality of your experiences and how they make you feel. The Ruthless educator exercises a mental muscle that sends him a signal prior to spiraling down the rabbit hole of Complacency. The challenge is in choosing to eventually spiral out of the negativity of complaining and into the productivity of assessing what you do and do not control. The mental muscle is just that—a muscle. You have to work it to strengthen it. The more you work at this, the better you'll become at spiraling in and out of negative cycles.

As a classroom teacher, this principle challenged me most when past teaching success didn't always portend future results. I began my career as a fourth-grade teacher. I was blessed to be at a brand-new school with plenty of resources, and supportive teammates. Our district recently adopted a new math program. I remember my teammates cautioning me not to be discouraged if students struggle because a steep learning curve for teachers and students was typical when new programs are adopted. As a brand-new teacher still smelling like baby powder, I wasn't discouraged by the warning, and appreciated the heads-up from my teammates.

I taught the hell out of that math content. The unit on fractions was dubbed as one where students would struggle mightily. You know that look students give you the moment they *get it?* Well, that was happening all over my classroom. If there was an audible "ping" sound for every student I reached, my classroom would sound like 10 Vegas slot machines hitting the jackpot simultaneously. Picture me moving from student to student in my class, lightly squeezing a sponge dipped in *the milk of mixed-fractions* just above each student's head and watching them absorb the milk and the learning. Regarding fourth grade mixed fractions, I looked in the mirror and saw a bad man.

Upon completion of that unit, I:

- gathered all my teaching materials
- placed them in a manila folder
- stored the folder in my tall filing cabinet for next year
- remembered I was an elementary teacher, and *laminated* the folder
- placed the folder back in my tall filing cabinet for next year

Fast forward to next year. I have a new group of fourth grade scholars and we've reached the unit covering mixed fractions. Without taking my eyes off of the students, I reach behind me, open the drawer of my tall file cabinet, feel around for the laminated folder, place it on the table and open it with a flourish! I arrange all my mixed-fractions magic tools like last year; same opening activities, engagement, hands-on opportunities, class work, homework, assessments, and feedback. I dipped the sponge in the warm milk of mixed-fractions mastery, and began teaching. I bet you can guess what happened next.

The milk had no magic, my instruction wasn't resonating, and everything that worked and earned me the awards I bestowed upon myself were bouncing off my student's heads like Teflon. It's one thing when you're struggling with pedagogy as a teacher. That's a signal for you to learn, grow, and improve. In my mind, I didn't fall into that category. I had great success teaching this unit. So, while reflecting on my practice didn't cross my mind, complaining about this year's class (of students) did cross my mind. I dove head first into a negative spiral. With the success of last school year, I had the perfect jumping off point for complaining about this year's students, and why *they* were the problem, and not *me*.

I blamed and complained for too long. Every minute I spent rationalizing and making excuses, was time that should've been devoted to seeking support or adding to my practice so I could respond to the learning styles of this year's students. Fortunately, I finally got a place where I knew I had to make adjustments with my instruction. As frustrated as I was, those circumstances couldn't compete with my teacher ego accepting the notion that I wasn't the primary influencer of student growth. I knew I had to change something.

This one experience shaped how I spiral in and out of problems. From that moment on, it's been my goal to reduce the span of time between *complaining* and *creating*. I'm human, and sometimes need to create space to feel and express frustration, how quickly can I go from *problem* to *productivity*. I apply this approach to all aspects of my life now. In the midst of beating myself up for something I've done, forgotten, or screwed up, there's a tiny coach on my shoulder whispering to me in between my self-flogging. This is how ruthless teachers build this muscle, and the strength of that muscle will be tested again and again over time.

COMPLACENCY AND BAG DRAGGERS

Do you know a colleague who has a pattern of arriving to work "dragged down by drama?" Not the person who's dealing with the rare unexpected crisis. I'm talking about the one who, when you see her turn the corner, heading down your hallway, it triggers inside you a deep sigh and mild panic. You sigh because you know what's following her, a big bag of drama. You panic because you know she's intent on "blessing you" with every detail of her drama. She is a:

BAG DRAGGER

No technology on earth can match the speed with which your mind is processing right now. Within three seconds, you're assessing your options:

Should I:

- shut off the lights and pretend I'm not here?
- grab my phone, pretend to call someone and just start talking?
- lie down and play dead?

Before you can decide, she's there, and you're done for. I call these energy vampires, **bag draggers.** Their behavior embodies one of the most draining forms of Complacency. It's after school, you've worked hard, and would like to make a few parent calls and get other work done before you leave for home. You saved up 38 brain cells from the day to make it happen, and Bag Dragging Bessie is coming for 39 of them. Bag draggers are first cousins of The Victim. Early in my career, I naively thought that some people just seemed to be unlucky and have so much going on in their lives. I was wrong.

Simply put, the difference between bag draggers and the rest of us is professional boundaries. When the professional shows up for work, her focus is on doing her job. But for bag draggers, there is no threshold, no boundaries. We all have things going on in our lives that could sabotage our work. Every educator falls somewhere on the spectrum from professional to Bag Dragger:

Level I: Professional: You deal with your bag of stuff at home, and leave it home as you make your way to work.

Level II: Professional: You set your bag of stuff on the passenger seat of your car. When you arrive at work, you leave the bag in your car, and head into the building.

Level III: Bag Dragger: You drag one bag of drama into the building, and share your "bag of blessings" with a *few* colleagues.

Level IV: Bag Dragger: You drag two bags of drama into the building, and share your "bags of blessings" with *several* colleagues.

Level V: Grand Poobah Bag Dragger: You drag your five-piece matching set of luggage into the building. You then "bless":

- anyone who'll listen
- anyone standing in place for longer than three seconds
- students feeling sick in the nurse's office
- students in in-school suspension
- UPS delivery drivers
- first grade students trying to deliver the lunch count to
- cafeteria staff
- angry parents waiting to see the principal

Any of this sound familiar?

Bag Dragging isn't simply a function of the drama in our lives; after all, we all have drama. It shows itself in the drama you allow to invade your work *at work*. Complacency as bag-dragging is not a victimless crime. The impact of the drama often results in work responsibilities you can't be expected to shoulder, and teammates who end up picking up your slack. Teaching is challenging enough when you show up and are fully present. It becomes more difficult when patterns of drama corrupt your work. It depletes and drains. It keeps you from doing the right work for yourself, your colleagues, and your students. If you're dragging bags, slide a bookmark here, and go throw those bags in the trunk of your car.

COMPLACENCY AND EXPENSIVE PEOPLE

Holding colleagues accountable is a challenge. It's a challenge when you only have a work relationship, and a challenge when you have close relationships. But there are colleagues stand out, the few who make you want to drink before saying anything to them. Why? Because you know their reaction to confrontation, constructive feedback, or accountability will be consistently over-the-top! The blowback you receive will be disproportionate to the issue you're addressing, and they make sure you pay a steep price for your professionalism. This is Complacency as:

EXPENSIVE PEOPLE

Expensive people use a weaponized form of Complacency. They force you into a dilemma that finds you at a crossroads moment where you're asking yourself: Is the value of confronting this issue worth the cost of the negative reaction? You're now vacillating about whether or not to broach an issue you know needs to be addressed. You're assessing the cost; rationalizing your decision not on its merits, but based on the personal cost. This cycle of doubt is all a part of Complacency's sorcery.

There are two types of Expensive People: **Hellraisers** and **Hurt Historians**.

- **Hellraisers** are the masters of overreaction. Their reaction is completely disproportionate to the severity of the issue. They know it, and their goal is for you to know it and learn from it. Your initial experience with a Hellraiser is shocking, and almost always results in you spending more time trying to de-escalate their response, and little time on the actual issue at hand. You'll come to dread confronting Hellraisers about anything. This is exactly what Hellraisers want you to do, and while they count it a victory, in the end, everyone loses.
- **Hurt Historians** take the courage you summoned to confront issues, turn the tables, and use history to make you feel horrible about addressing the issue. The Hurt Historian seeks to avoid real-time confrontation by distracting you with how you've done them wrong throughout history. They love using

absolute sentence starters like *you always* and *every time I.* Rather than deal with an issue in real time, they draw on history to point out your imperfections and foibles, ultimately leading you down a path that ends with you feeling like the one at fault. The Hurt Historian is committed to this strategy, so issues aren't addressed or resolved.

With both types, you'll often find yourself apologizing for your actions. Your logical side knows you're not in the wrong, but your emotional side is understandably ready to wave the white flag and end this journey to nowhere.

Of course, the solution isn't to simply avoid addressing issues with expensive people, or addressing everything with them. There is a sweet spot. Here is the thought process I employ when dealing with expensive people:

1. *Reflect, evaluate, and decide if the issue warrants being confronted.* It's a delicate form of *picking your battles* because the *expense* can't be a part of your equation.

2. *Clarify communication outcomes.* I can't control the outcome of the confrontation, only I what I communicate. I get clear on exactly what I need to say, down to the wording. And I rehearse it enough because I know I'm going to be confronted with the distraction and diversions of history and overreaction. While it would be great if the confrontation was productive, my mission is to focus on the part I control: clearly communicating my concerns.

3. *Proceed with if/then courage.* When I find myself thinking too much about the price of confrontation, I think to myself, *if* this person is bold enough to distract me with their reaction, *then* I have to be bold enough to confront the issue.

The challenge is to say what needs to be said, while not owning their response, which is much easier said than done. Expensive people want their overreaction to be a lesson for you. They seek to inflict enough mental trauma so as to make you think twice about confronting them next time.

RUTHLESS EQUITY TEACHERS ILLUMINATE

Take a look at the imagery on the cover of this book. It shows one illuminated lightbulb taking off. This represents both a willingness to disrupt the status-quo, and a willingness to illuminate. Educators must strike the balance between disruption and inclusion. It's not enough to just march to a different beat; you also have an obligation to show your light. That light will attract others to align with you. You've got to be open, transparent, and generous with strategies, resources, and practices that are working for you, as well as the ones that aren't yielding desired results. This is a deficit area in our field. Not only are educators hesitant to illuminate the path, but also reluctant to connect their instructional practice to student learning results.

In their book, *Removing Labels*, Smith and colleagues cite research conducted by Evans et al. that noted, when teachers examine students' assessment data over the course of a school year, they tend to attribute performance to student characteristics rather than their own teaching. Fully eighty-five percent of teacher explanations focused on:

- student behavior (e.g., "not paying attention"),
- a mismatch between the assessment demands and the student (e.g., "he's an English language learner"),
- students' home life (e.g., "they don't read at home"),
- or suspected or established underlying conditions (e.g., "I think she's dyslexic").

Teachers' explanations focused on instruction only fifteen percent of the time. What is particularly troubling is that many of the explanations were based on perceptions and assumptions, specifically as they related to home life and underlying conditions. Some of these may in fact be the case. Smith et al go further and assert that educators need to "differentiate between teachers' claims about students that are verifiable and those that are subjective, particularly negative, opinions about children." This sobering data underscores a collective crisis of confidence in teachers.

Smith and his colleagues go further and speculate that because educators don't feel successful with students they view as lower achieving, they subconsciously avoid contact with them. As humans, we have a natural yearning to surround ourselves with people who make us feel good about ourselves. This is true in social and professional settings. Students struggling to make academic gains make us feel like failures, so unconsciously, it can create detachment. Awareness of this is so important because left unchecked, it ensures a widening of the gap between students perceived as capable and those perceived as less capable. In economic terms, the rich get richer, while the poor get poorer. The impact of teacher expectations and teacher self-efficacy cannot be understated.

RUTHLESS TEACHERS ARE ADVOCATES, NOT SAVIORS

Dr. Rosa Perez-Isiah is an author, a speaker, a consultant, and an Elementary School Director of Equity and Access at Norwalk La Mirada Unified School District in California. She has a powerful perspective on the issue of the Savior Complex. "Educators often become consumed by the challenges that some of our students face, including poverty, adverse childhood experiences, and injustice. The worst thing we can do for students is fall into the sympathy-for-my-babies trap. Our students need our empathy, not sympathy. They need us to understand their plight and to provide them with the knowledge and tools needed to succeed."

The Savior Complex in education, often held by well-intentioned educators, is the belief that one should save "poor kids" or "poor babies," especially when working with underserved and marginalized groups. A savior feels that they have knowledge and power that must be bestowed upon the students instead of creating opportunities to empower students to learn at high levels.

We cannot control the effects of poverty and other challenging or traumatic experiences. What we do control is what we do for students every day. Students need passionate advocates and high expectations with support, great teaching, empathy, and rigor. Focusing your time, energy, and resources in these areas requires ruthlessness. Loving students and having high-expectations for them are not mutually exclusive. You can do both. You must do both! Don't pity them, promise them! Our students need warriors who commit to Ruthless Equity.

This is about mindset. Here are some indicators to help you recognize the difference between **savior mode** and **advocate mode**: When student poverty, adversity, and challenges move you to:

- protect them from the challenges of rigor because of what they're going through outside of school, you're doing **charity** work.
- feel urgency to close learning gaps and move them to grade-level or better performance, you're doing **advocacy** work.
- lower expectations to make them feel successful, you're doing **charity** work.
- be more innovative with instruction without compromising learning expectations, you're doing **advocacy** work.
- lower learning expectations because you associate poverty with intelligence, you're doing **charity** work.
- mine for students' strengths so you can use them to build underdeveloped skill areas, you're doing **advocacy** work.
- expect and demand less due to student circumstances, you're doing **charity** work.
- provide scaffolds for grade-level or better success, you're doing **advocacy** work.
- Advocacy work is teaching the *student* and not the *circumstance*.

COMPLACENCY AND MARGINALIZING LABELS

Complacency loves when you use labels to marginalize students. These labels result in you calibrating your expectations of students. Before the ink is dry on the class roster, Complacency is highlighting challenges and deficits. As if on autopilot, Complacency helps the teacher form fixed conclusions about his students. Before the teacher ever meets them, Complacency has gift-wrapped excuses such as:

We've become numb to the labels. They roll off our tongues and stick to students like tattoos. I invite you and your colleagues to participate in this activity. Using one of the three labels in the graphic below, evaluate each of your colleagues, and write their name in the column aligned with your assessment. By the way, you don't get to place everyone in the high-ability column.

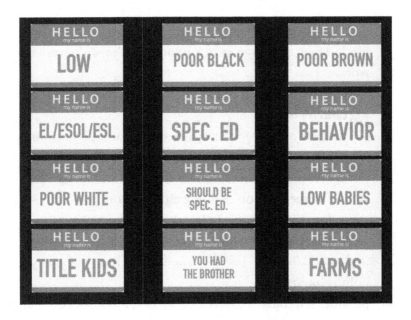

High Ability Teachers	Avg Ability Teachers	Low Ability Teachers

After you're done, imagine the results being shared at the next staff meeting and displayed in the school's data room, alongside student data. Need I say more?

The teacher is about to earn Complacency's Triple Crown by ranking, sorting, and selecting his students. He's already identified the "high kids," the "average students," and "the low group." In his mind, these factors outside his control have more leverage than anything he can do. Here's the unseen tragedy of this approach. When you lower your expectations based on those factors, you're giving students license to use these excuses as well. You are contributing to the creation a new generation of victims.

While there have been many experimental studies done around teacher expectations, the findings of Rosenthal and Jacobson in 1968 are still regarded as the landmark. Smith et al. summarize the results and note that student achievement could rise and fall depending on teachers' expectations of their learners. When teachers expected students to excel based on fictitious prior achievement data they believed to be true, the student performed at high levels. The reverse was also true. When teachers were given false low prior achievement data, the students did not perform as well. Again, this highlights the power of teacher expectations and a woeful lack of teacher self-efficacy as well. What chance do students have when teachers don't regard their work as a significant determinant of student performance?

THE RUTHLESS AND THE LOW

At my school, teachers referring to our students as "low" was an embedded part of our school culture. While I understood why they thought this way, each "low" reference frustrated me more and more. My retort, "We don't have low students," wasn't enough to shift their thinking. In the long run, I knew that improved student learning results would help with the needed shift. But in the short run, I needed to plant some "mindset seeds." So, when I met with teacher teams and the familiar "low student" lament bubbled to the surface, I would interrupt with the following:

- Me (principal): When I hear you refer to your students as "low," it signals to me that I have failed you.
- Teacher(s): (looking confused) What makes you say that?
- Me (principal): Well, when you say your students are "low," I interpret it as you saying, "our team is low." I hear you saying, "our team doesn't have the supports, resources, creativity, and collective expertise to ensure learning for these kids." My job is to provide you with resources, supports, and tools so when you don't believe your team has the goods to make learning happen, that is my failure.

My teachers didn't like that at all, and some were even offended. But it was the truth. Challenging the status-quo created productive discomfort, and I challenged this paradigm. The "low" label renders students incapable of learning at high levels, and teachers incapable of recognizing student strengths. I didn't back off this notion, and eventually, with improved efficacy and results, there was a shift in teacher thinking and teacher efficacy at our school.

IF YOU CALL THEM LOW, YOU'LL TEACH THEM LOW.

No educator has ever referred to a student as "low" and expected him to learn at high levels. Have an honest conversation with yourself. What marginalizing labels are currently used to *define* your students?

I work with many educators who scoff at the "low" label, but instead of getting rid of it, they cleverly replace "low" with more palatable and equally damaging labels such as:

- cusp kids
- trailer-park kids
- apartment kids
- kids from (that street or that side of town)
- Title-I Kids
- struggling learners
- minorities
- poor kids

You can't have a culture of *learning for all* while some students receive below-grade-level instruction all year long. Your students know when you believe they're dumb, without you ever saying it.

Thomas Good's research reveals how teacher expectations lead to a significant difference in interactions based on whether students were perceived as high-or low-performing. In particular, students perceived as low performing:

- are criticized more often for failure,
- are praised less frequently,
- receive less feedback,
- are called on less often,
- are seated farther away from the teacher,
- have less eye contact from the teacher,
- have fewer friendly interactions with the teacher,
- and experience acceptance of their ideas less often.

Smith et al. cite Hall & Sandler's term for this: a "chilly" classroom climate, in which some students do not feel they are valued and instead that "their presence…is at best peripheral, and at worst an unwelcome intrusion." Connecting these findings back to the need for belonging and inclusion, how can we expect the best of students when they receive these messages on a daily basis?

When you lower expectations because your heart hurts for their situation, you're treating your students like charity cases, and your instruction is a benevolent favor to them. It's the worst message to send them, and it can cripple them for life.

Teacher expectations are the primary determinant of student success. We have to chip away at that sobering statistic from earlier showing that teachers attribute about fifteen percent of student learning results to their influence. This begins with mining for their strengths and gifts, which is rarely considered with students tattooed with "low" labels. You cannot allow labels to determine student destiny.

WHEN YOU REFER TO STUDENTS AS LOW, THE BEST THEY CAN HOPE FOR IS YOU GROWING THEM TO A HIGHER LEVEL OF LOW.

THE COURAGE TO GROUP DIFFERENTLY

There exists an inherent conflict between equitable practices and ability grouping. Ensuring equity requires a focus on essential learning outcomes students must master to be successful at:

1. the next grade-level,
2. the next course,
3. the high-stakes assessment (where applicable) and,
4. life beyond the K-12 system

With equity for all as the goal, how can students be taught below grade-level all year long? Ability groups have existed in schools for more than a century. They're created based on educator perceptions of student intelligence or the results of a standardized test. They're fortified by the staying power of the debunked "bell-shaped curse." In education, ability is regarded as finite—you either have it, or you don't. Think back to your own days as a student. Students sentenced to low groups remained in low groups throughout their school career. Students placed in average or high groups stayed in the same groups year after year.

That's because these groups are based on fixed mindset thinking. I removed the word *ability* from my teacher vocabulary and replaced it with *performance*. Because ability is *finite*, and performance can be *improved*.

Reject the trap of inflexible ability grouping. This is Complacency dressed as fixed mindset. If you affix "low" labels to students, then you're off the hook for innovating, creating, and collaborating around building scaffolds that lead every student to grade-level (or higher) success. The thinking is, *Low students can't be expected to do grade-level work, so let's meet them where they are and hope they just grow some.*

Honors For All

Ann Campbell is a World History teacher in Irvine, California. She's part of a team that decided to be ruthless about equity and access for every student. Ann shares her journey: "This year at University High School, we dismantled ability groups for freshmen in our Global Perspectives (World History) courses. Prior to this year, we segregated students into CP (College Prep—the minimum requirement for graduation and college acceptance)—and Honors level classes. For a few years we had been informally discussing offering only one level with an embedded Honors Distinction program. Last January, I once again mentioned the idea to my administrator and we decided since our educational world was already upside down with COVID restrictions, so why not go for it."

"We put a plan in place and changed our program in the fall of 2021. The benefits were immediately evident. As one of my colleagues put it, 'Both groups have strengths, and we put all those strengths together.' One of my favorite success stories is a student named Andre. Andre is brilliant but does not know he is brilliant. Now to be fair, he's been a non-producer...not much work makes it into the grade book, but we are working on that. However, Andre is a regular participant in class discussions and what I noticed very early on is he understands the content; not just basic recall, but the deeper level nuances of historical events."

"Andre is a critical thinker. On one particular day we were practicing "Academic Discourse," an activity in which I explicitly teach the students how to engage in content discussions by elevating their academic vocabulary and working on speaking in complex sentences. I give sentence starters and key vocabulary they can use. The topic for the day was weighty...we were analyzing the differences between Capitalism, Socialism and Communism. After a small-group discussion, I asked for volunteers to share their thoughts. Andre raised his hand and explained "Socialism is when the government allocates funds to distribute to citizens to ensure everyone lives a quality life." When I heard those words, I could have cried. I was so proud of Andre and I knew at that moment our hard work, and our vision to provide equity and opportunity to ALL students was paying off and was the right thing to do."

The decision to take the risk in disrupting the status-quo of ability grouping makes my heart sing. And, I love that Ann keeps it real. She acknowledges that Andre still has some things to work on, i.e.: handing in work. And she *expects* him to get there, it's the next rung up the ladder. Ann is a warm demander. What also impresses me is how Ann and her team regarded the upheaval and chaos of COVID as an *opportunity*, and not a *hindrance*. Andre and all other students will benefit from the decision to disrupt. For them, and the team of teachers, this decision turned out to be a gift of Covid.

Giving Covid the Credit

Guiding Question: In what ways are you better as a result of navigating the challenges of the global pandemic?

FROM CHARITY TEACHER TO EQUITY ADVOCATE

How does Ruthless Equity address students who are performing below grade-level or better? Well, the answer makes clear the difference between you being a charity worker and an advocate. First is the fundamental assumption that your school's schedule provides for extra time and support for students to master essential learning outcomes, and extension/enrichment support for students who've mastered the outcome before others. With that in mind, here's the critical mindset distinction between charity and advocacy.

> **Scenario:** 5th Grade Mathematics Essential Learning Outcome: *Fluently multiply multi-digit whole numbers using the standard algorithm.*

> **Allotted Time Frame for Mastery:** Three Weeks

You have students performing below grade-level as it relates to this standard. They haven't progressed past multiplying one digit by one digit.

THE TEACHER AS CHARITY WORKER

You know you're doing charity work when you "meet students where they are" and your best hope is that they "grow a little." Your heart is in the right place in that you want to "move them" further along, but your expectations are low because "further along" is ambiguous, and not grade-level or better. Your goal is for them to just "grow a little bit."

With this approach, you're "doing students a favor." This is charity work. These limitations you've placed on what you believe they *can* and *cannot* learn aren't based on your strengths and gifts, but your biases, fixed mindset, and lack of efficacy. You not only stunt student growth, but your own as well. It's impossible for you to be at your best as a teacher when you don't believe you have the knowledge, skills and resources to ensure learning. In the end, you're working hard and hoping you can nudge them just ahead of where they started. *Your focus is firmly fixed on where students are, not where they need to go (grade-level or better).*

THE TEACHER AS RUTHLESS EQUITY ADVOCATE

Let's revisit charity work and advocacy work in more detail. You know you're doing advocacy work when you "meet students where they are" and while there, gaze upward and lock in on where they have to go (grade-level or better). With advocacy work, both your heart (intention) and your hands (practice) are in the right place. When you meet students where they are with an eye fixed on the essential learning outcome, it triggers an urgency with pacing that moves you to right action:

1. You assess the current reality and share the results with your student. You show him where he is today (one by one multiplication) and where he has to go (fluent multi-digit multiplication).

2. You make a declaration that you're going to work together to ensure he masters the essential learning outcome. You don't hide the fact that it's going to be challenging. You make it clear that you're going to marshal the necessary resources, you believe in him, and he *will* achieve it by the time frame you've established for all students to achieve mastery of the standard.

3. You consider all of the most critical prerequisite skills and competencies that make up the learning gap.

4. The established timeframe of three weeks will cause you to evaluate and place a value on the missing prerequisite skills and competencies. It's often impossible to teach all the missing skills, so you then determine:

   • Which missing skills are most important to make up?

- Which skills have "leverage" and will benefit the student in multiple areas?
- Which missing skills will create the most efficient direct path to mastery of the essential learning outcome?
- What resources can I access?
- What enriching preview experiences can I provide students?
- Who can help me with devising and executing this plan?

Do you feel the difference between *charity* and *advocacy?* With charity, you're doing a little more than just feeling sorry for your student. Your intention for him is to learn...*something.* Advocacy creates strategic urgency. Like Cosmequity, the charity teacher can create optics that make him difficult to detect. Both the teacher as charity worker and the teacher as advocate work hard, which is why I bristle when a teacher's retort to recommended changes in practice is, "We're working so hard!" This is true, but "working hard" isn't the outcome of our work, ensuring learning is the outcome. And since you're working hard, don't you want your results to be a reflection of your hard work?

The Intersection of Charity and Advocacy

Guiding Question: Does your work with students align more with charity or advocacy?

THE RUTHLESS EQUITY TEACHER IS NOT DATA-DRIVEN

Did your head just do a 360-degree turn? Not data-driven? C'mon, man! That's the chorus of one of education's most beloved hymns! Our relentless focus on being *data-driven* has resulted in "looking at data (data-driven)" becoming the outcome of our work. I've worked with many schools that devote precious energy, time, and effort into analyzing data; The End. When teaching-learning-assessment cycle ends for these learning outcomes, it's clear that the finish line has been identified as analyzing data rather than ensuring mastery of essential learning outcomes.

RUTHLESS EQUITY TEACHERS ARE DATA INFORMED AND RESULTS ORIENTED.

WHAT DO YOUR EYES TELL THEM?

When students walk into your classroom, their first concern isn't whether they'll master today's posted learning objective. Their first concern involves you. They look at you and wonder:

DO I BELIEVE S(HE) BELIEVES IN ME?

What do your eyes tell your students? What they conclude is based on your expectations of them.

Do I Believe She Believes In Me?

Guiding Question: What do you do to make your students know you believe in them?

THE COURAGE TO GO FOR IT!

You have to be *all-in* on mission. You're closing the door on Complacency and its many built-in excuses for why some students can't learn. You're taking those excuses and turning them into context for how you will respond. This is a paradigm shift from traditional schooling, where we decide which students can and can't. You're going against the grain. This takes courage to do while navigating both the reactions of colleagues and your fear of failure.

When you emerge from your first round of Ruthless Equity in mindset and practice, you're going to feel like a superhero. Disrupting the status-quo narrative will fuel you. With every round of this process, you'll become more powerful. In the mirror, you'll see a teacher who is unstoppable.

I know what you're thinking...*Ken, I want to be Ruthless, but how do I make it happen with students who are performing below grade-level in several areas?* It's a great question and a real concern. Ann Campbell and her teammates at University High provided us with one point of entry. The rest of this chapter will help disrupt old patterns and stretch your thinking. It's all in preparation for the next chapter, which is dedicated to dismantling ability groups, and showcasing student brilliance. We'll explore a point of entry that creates a shift in mindset, practice, and is universal, so it can be applied by every teacher, in every content area, and to the benefit of every student.

RUTHLESS REMINDERS

- Disrupting the status-quo takes courage.

- Victimhood isn't a victimless crime.

- Some colleagues will change when you become ruthless.

- Ruthless teachers illuminate, and light the path for others to follow.

- There is a fine line between advocacy and charity.

- Marginalizing labels and ability groups are inequitable practices and cannot co-exist in a culture of Ruthless Equity.

- You must examine your grouping practices in light of its impact on your ability to ensure equity.

- Look for the opportunities offered by obstacles.

- Teach the student, not the label.

- Marginalizing labels violate dignity and dehumanize students.

RUTHLESS REFLECTIONS

With a team of colleagues, discuss the following questions:

What are the grouping practices in place in your classroom?

_____

_____

_____

What marginalizing labels are used in your practice?

_____

_____

_____

In your experience as a student, what labels were used to *define* you?

_____

_____

_____

How have your beliefs and practices changed at this point of the book?

_____

_____

_____

CHAPTER SIX

THE SECOND RULE OF RUTHLESSNESS
A COMMITMENT TO:
DISMANTLING ABILITY GROUPS

Ensuring equity requires you to confront the long-standing inequitable practice of ability groups, often referred to as tracking. With so many schools making S.E.L. (social emotional learning) a priority, ability groups represent an SEL opportunity because ability groups negatively impact the social and emotional well-being of students, and sentence students to below grade-level instruction.

NOTHING KILLS PROBLEM-SOLVING FASTER THAN FOCUSING ON WHAT YOU CANNOT CONTROL.

THE BULLY RETREATS

Why does Complacency give way when we become Ruthless? Because Complacency is a textbook bully, a punk. Remember what we learned about Pennywise? Complacency has no strength of its own; its power is derived entirely from our fear of it. Once a bully sees you stiffen your back and stand tall, his feet begin to shuffle nervously, and he gives ground. Just as sure as the sun rises, the ruthless educator keeps coming and coming. She beats Complacency at its own game by being even more relentless and indomitable than it is.

Ability-grouping is a stubborn bully we're guilty of keeping alive. Despite decades of research decrying the practice, the embracing of growth mindset, ability grouping seems to rise from the rubble every time. Ability grouping not only marginalizes students, but teachers as well because it results in the downward calibration of expectations. This practice frames student learning as already determined, permanent, limited, and finite.

Conversely, in a culture of equity, student learning is fluid; existing at a performance level that can be improved with teacher guidance and support. Upending the paradigm of ability grouping can appear daunting. And I know that dismantling ability groups requires more than attitude and sheer will. We must fight fire with fire, and replace ability grouping with a more powerful equitable option.

DISMANTLING ABILITY GROUPS, IN MINDSET AND PRACTICE

Georgina Rivera is a teacher, coach, and consultant in education. She also serves as vice president of the National Council of Teachers in Mathematics. Georgina produces transformational results from her commitment to both equitable mindset and practices. I conducted an interview with her to discuss dismantling ability groups. One of her strengths is taking the research, applying it to practice, and delivering content in a way that's both practical and empowering.

I have divided the interview content into passages reflection prior to moving to the next topic. I asked Rivera to explain the process of dismantling ability groups in the classroom. The remainder of this chapter outlines one powerful process she uses. Included is the testimony of a teacher she coaches, and how the alternative has both improved her teaching practice and student learning.

The term *paradigm shift* has almost become cliché in education. But I don't know of another term that aptly describes the monumental shift in thinking, practice, and belief required to dismantle ability groups. I am floored by the number of schools and districts claiming a commitment to equity while ability grouping remains a prominent policy and practice.

We can't expect real change from exposing *why* the practice is so damaging, if it's not followed by *how* to create the change. A change in practice alone only engages the *hands*. To bring about transformative change, your *hands*, your *head* and your *heart* must be engaged as well, working in concert.

Lastly, Georgina uses mathematics as the context to explain the process, and acknowledges how this is universal practice, and can be modified for every content area. Let's dig in!

DISMANTLING ABILITY GROUPS STARTS WITH THE WHY

"Changing an embedded practice like ability grouping is going to be challenging. Ironically, the heaviest lifting is to change the mindset behind the practice, not the practice itself. Trying to make this kind of change without making the case for why almost guarantees it will die on the vine. So, let's start with *why*."

"The label, *ability group* is inherently problematic. It already implies that some students are able and some are not. From the outset, the notion that some students are capable and some aren't already sets up an uneven playing field and sets some students up to not receive grade-level content. The label is rooted in deficit thinking that proves damaging to students at both ends of the perceived spectrum."

"The labels we use feel like a lifelong sentence that's bad on both ends. For students perceived to have high ability, it often triggers the assumption that students know perhaps more than they do, and learn *everything* with ease. So many students feel anxiety because they're expected to already know the content. I've worked with many students with the *high group* label who develop anxiety because they're embarrassed when they struggle with a concept or have a question. This is a form of fixed mindset thinking that we do to students."

"For students labeled as low, it immediately prompts teachers to look for what students can't do, don't know, and what they lack. When these labels stick, there's no way out for students. The ability group label automatically creates a culture driven by deficit thinking that makes it impossible to ensure high levels of learning. When teachers are focused on what students lack, it deprives them of discovering each students' individual strengths and gifts."

ABILITY GROUPING CREATES IDENTITY DIM

"As a classroom teacher I look for the brilliance in kids. Unfortunately, our classrooms were often arranged by ability group. Students who may struggle in specific areas, but also have strengths in other areas were sentenced to the low group, and they would take the label on as their identity as a learner. Students think, "I'm in the low group so I'm going to perform as if I'm low." The low label becomes how they identify as learners. I could see their brilliance dim before my eyes. I couldn't change how classes were structured at our school, so my journey in this work began with me being intentional about giving my students more rigorous tasks, often the same tasks reserved for students in accelerated classes, but in my mind, they are all brilliant. Time after time, students relegated to the low group never ceased to amaze me! They rise to the occasion and find a way to shine. There was no doubt in my mind that our students could do the work."

"Systems built around ability are rooted in a deficit belief system. The danger is it's often built on a single story; sometimes in the form of assessment results, and other times, a story shared by colleagues. Too often, none of it is set in real evidence that is deep enough to understand the whole child."

DISCOVER EACH STUDENTS' LEARNER-IDENTITY

"Over time, I noticed students had either a positive math identity or a negative math identity. I'd hear things like, *I am a math person* or *I'm not a math person* and that identity would play out in assessments and the way they would approach learning tasks. Your learner identity affects how you engage in learning, and what you believe you can accomplish."

"Along with building community and getting to know my kids, I'd also spend the first month of the school year discovering what each student's learner-identity is. I gain awareness of how students engaged during learning, their level of confidence, and willingness to advocate for themselves. I learned how each student approached challenges. Did they attack the learning or shy away? Ability groups make it almost impossible to tap into student strengths."

THE GROUPING DILEMMA

Education has evolved from the traditional arrangement of students seated in rows and working individually, to group work becoming a staple in classrooms. Peter Liljedahl, author of *Building Thinking Classrooms in Mathematics* provides insights on the grouping dilemma; in most cases, the formation of groups is either a strategically planned arrangement decided by the teacher, or self-selected groups decided by students—each of which offers different affordances. The strategically arranged classroom allows the teacher to maintain control over who works together and, often more importantly, who doesn't work together. In so doing she constructs, in her mind, an optimal environment for achieving her goals for the lesson. Likewise, if the students are allowed to decide who they will work with, they will invariably make such decisions strategically in the pursuit of achieving their goals for the lesson. In either case, the specific grouping of the students offers different affordances in the attainment of these, often disparate, goals.

When teachers group students with learning outcomes in mind, there's a specific arrangement she believes will allow students to learn best from one another. Liljedahl found when a teacher groups students in order to be productive, she is looking for groupings that lead to the completion of more work. This may, for example, require there to be a strong leader in a group for project work. It may also mean that friends or weak students do not sit together, as such pairings may lead to less productivity. Groupings designed to maintain peace and order in the classroom would prompt the teacher to not put 'trouble-makers' together, as their antics may be disruptive to the other learners in the class. Interestingly, students may self-select themselves into groupings for the same aforementioned reasons. So, it's easy to see how group formation from the teacher and student perspective can have conflicting goals. Are you ready for the *what if?*

THE POWER OF VISIBLY RANDOMIZED GROUPS

What if there was a grouping practice that could bring together the often-disparate grouping goals of both teachers and students? A grouping practice that can lead to:

1. students becoming agreeable to work in any group they are placed in
2. the *elimination* of social barriers within the classroom
3. an *increase* in the mobility of knowledge between students
4. a *decrease* in reliance on the teacher for answers
5. an *increase* in the reliance on co-constructed intra-and inter-group answers
6. an *increase* in both enthusiasm for mathematics class and engagement in mathematics tasks, and
7. the permanent eradication of ability groups

What if the selection of groups was not made strategically—by either party? What if it was left up to chance—done randomly—with no attention paid to the potential benefits that specific groupings could offer either a teacher or a learner? The Visibly Random Groups practice was developed by Peter Liljedahl. Georgina Rivera and fifth-grade teacher Julia Darcy, are going to share the impact of this powerful practice. Georgina shares from a leadership and coach perspective. Then, Julia will share how the practice impacts her classroom.

"First, you have to commit to the practice of randomized groupings on a daily basis. It must be visible to students that they can be grouped with any student at any time. Students must see and know that you've not arranged the groups or manipulated the system. Over time, it sends them the message that you believe they're capable of engaging with any group of their peers. I need to emphasize that groupings must be visibly random. Students must see and know that you're not arranging groups or manipulating the system. Once the random nature of grouping is confirmed, we saw a huge difference in student mindset and identity because they know no one has *placed* them in that group. Every student is in a group solely because of the card selected."

THE ROLE OF NO ROLES

"Second, it is critical that we not assign roles to students, because it throws students right back into assuming identities. When students are assigned a role, the dynamics of the group revert back to traditional methods of grouping. Traditional grouping practices for the *few*, not the *many*. So, instead of taking roles like: I'*m the student expected to record for the group* or, *I'm expected to speak up most of the time or, I'm the student that keeps the time for the group,* you'll discover that they figure it out, and they figure it out fast. When there's a group that is stuck, it's an opportunity to walk over, help the group, and move on. Even with the randomness, groups getting stuck is more the exception than the rule, and sometimes the groups get the issues before I arrive to provide support."

SHIFT IDENTITY WITH SMALL MEANINGFUL WINS

"Small meaningful wins lay a foundation by engaging students with tasks that are both rigorous and accessible to all students. This isn't to be interpreted as *dumbing down* in any way, in fact, it's quite the opposite. For some students, it reinforces the notion that everyone is capable. For other students, the strategy reinforces that, *I am capable*, and *I belong here.*"

"At the beginning, this may take a little planning, but it's doable. Again, the task should be both challenging and accessible to all students. Here's an example of a small meaningful win:

HOW MANY TIMES DOES THE DIGIT SEVEN APPEAR BETWEEN ONE AND ONE-HUNDRED?

An extension might be:

HOW MANY TIMES DOES THE DIGIT SEVEN APPEAR BETWEEN ONE AND ONE-THOUSAND?

While this isn't a complex problem to solve, the answer also isn't sitting on the tip of anyone's tongue. So, solving it requires thinking and effort, and every student can engage in a process to figure out the solution. Every student can engage this task. Significant prior knowledge isn't required, nor does it require explanation of context because they're just manipulating digits."

"Arranging students in randomized groups, providing each student with vertical surfaces or whiteboards, and then standing back to watch them explore, collaborate, and share their individual and group work is a sight to behold. Often without prompting, there develops a very powerful and humanizing appreciation for different ways of thinking, processing and solving. As a reminder, I'm using math as my lens for explaining this process, but visibly random groups can be adapted for *every* content area."

SHOWCASING STUDENT BRILLIANCE

"Visibly Random Groups showcase brilliance from across the room because there's a *mobility of knowledge,* where students learn from each other because they're a community and because every day they're with a different group of peers. With no roles about who each person is *supposed* to be, there's always an opportunity to learn from someone new. In a class of twenty-five students, I have twenty-five potential peer tutors who can share their knowledge with me and their classmates."

"When teachers express concerns about standards they don't know, missed learning or learning loss, I explain that you're going to find exactly what you look for. As a classroom teacher if you focus on what kids don't know, you'll find that there is a lot students don't know. I'm not dismissing learning gaps; I'm making a case for the lens worn while engaging this work. If you choose to see everything through a deficit lens, then you'll find all the deficit evidence you need to justify not providing students with this opportunity. If you approach teaching through the lens focused on capitalizing on what students do know, you're going to find that students are able to do and learn more than you expected."

NOT ALL LEARNING IS DONE ON LADDERS

"There is a notion that learning is a ladder. In other words, every mathematics skill requires mastery of prerequisite skills. The learning ladder notion turns out to be a false narrative that creates cognitive dissonance for teachers when the practice of teaching all students at grade-level or better is brought to the table. While some learning requires prerequisites, it's not as universal as we think. With students having so many potential sources of information, knowledge, enrichment, and exposure, much of learning in today's world looks less like a ladder and more like an interconnected web. There are many instances when you don't have to know one standard to work on another standard. As an example, I've worked with students able to multiply fractions with ease, but then struggle with adding fractions. Conventional thinking would reason those students who aren't able to add fractions should not be able to multiply fractions. However, I've worked with students who fit this profile. Many students struggle with addition of fractions because there's actually more of a cognitive load on the process because of the amount of work required."

"There's a place in the randomized grouping practice to fill in necessary gaps. However, the success of the practice hinges on the lens you wear as a teacher. If you wear a deficit lens and try to always teach backwards, you're widening this gap, which is often the evidence used to maintain ability grouping as a practice. If you're always teaching backwards, then when do you ever get to teach what's essential? That's why the dismantling of ability groups through visibly random grouping is critical for your mindset as a teacher, but for student mindset as well."

"When you commit to the practice of visibly random groups, you'll see students perform at consistently higher level. Over time, this practice will become *the way we do things around here.* That's the vision we have for our school."

PREPARING STUDENTS FOR LIFE

"Moving from ability groups to visibly random groups prepares students for real life! In life, you work with different people, who know different things, who are from different cultures, and may have a different approach to meeting goals. Randomized grouping mimics life, and creates the space for equity, networking, skillful listening, collaboration, and belonging. Visibly random groups help students break down social barriers, and learn about one another; two skills needed as they navigate the demands of the 21st century."

TEACHER AS COACH

"As you're walking the room and watching groups work, if you notice a common learning misconception, you pause all the groups, put the learning issue on display, and address it whole group. If you notice individual students struggling, you intervene based on the misconception, *not their label.* I encourage our teachers to coach. Don't rescue, save, or pity students. Coach them. I love when our teachers intervene with a student and say: "I pulled you aside to give you a coaching move. Here's what I want you to think about...""

"One of the greatest gifts of this practice is how it's removed the stress of *leveling the learning*. We no longer are burdened with creating a lower curricular track, an average track and an advanced track. Our approach is teaching every student at grade-level or better. We're seeing a significant reduction in the percentage of students working below grade-level, and a sharp increase in the percentage of students working at or above proficiency levels! Everybody wins!"

EVERY DAY I'M SHUFFLIN'

Julia Darcy, the 5th grade teacher who shared the Identity Work going on at Greene Hills School, has doubled-down and embedded visibly random groups in her classroom. She shares some of the highlights and benefits of visibly randomized groups.

VISIBLY RANDOM GROUPS: OBSERVATIONS AND RESULTS

"When I heard the idea and read about it, I jumped right in and started the year off with the strategy. It took about two weeks to really see the power of it. I have a deck of cards and hand one to teach student as they enter the classroom. The four students holding the queen cards gather together in one area, and the four students holding cards with the number 9 gather in another area. The process continues until every student is part of a group. It's important that students see the randomness."

"Students know that sometimes you're going to be in a group where one of your peers might need your help, and other times when you're the student who needs the help. Each group is provided vertical white-board space so they can show and explain their thinking. Regardless of performance level, random grouping and access points are key so that everyone student feels valued. Every student knows they have something to add to the conversation."

"Our classroom culture is now one where students see the value of learning with each other. They understand we all have things to learn, and each of us brings a unique perspective to learning. They understand that while they may have the correct answer, their partner may approach the problem in a different way. I've learned there's so much power when you remove roles. Visibly Random Groups have made the largest positive impact on student learning and classroom culture this year (mic drop)."

Georgina and Julia's work with randomized grouping and Ann Campbell's work with providing every student access to honors-level courses are two examples of disrupting the status-quo around grouping practices. My intention is to plant seeds for what's possible. In the next chapter, we're going to take a deeper dive into this work through the heart, head, and hands of another model *Ruthless Equity* educator.

IF STUDENTS DON'T KNOW THEMSELVES, OTHERS WILL TELL THEM WHO THEY ARE, IN WAYS THAT MAY NOT BE POSITIVE OR ACCURATE. —GHOLDY MUHAMMED, AUTHOR, *CULTIVATING GENIUS: AN EQUITY FRAMEWORK FOR CULTURALLY AND HISTORICALLY RESPONSIVE LITERACY*

MY TWO

Sister Mary Claire, my second-grade teacher, gets credit for my first encounter with a teacher who embodied Ruthless Equity. She was and still is magic! As a teacher, she was relational, a warm demander, funny, and did everything with a kind and gentle spirit. She made me feel like a million bucks! She made me believe I could do anything! Granted, my parents told me I could do anything, but parents are supposed to tell you that. Sister Mary Claire combined relational warmth with high-expectations. I was challenged, stretched, encouraged, and coached.

On one occasion, Sister Mary Claire visited my home, which was located in a neighborhood where everyone looked like me, and no one looked like her. The visit was a positive one, though today we laugh because neither she nor I can recall exactly why she visited. I also cannot recall the exact conversation between her and my mother. I do remember, however, exactly where she sat, and most importantly, how I felt. To this day, nearly fifty years later, I can close my eyes and be back at my childhood home, watching *my* teacher talk about me in glowing terms to my mother. All these years later, I still levitate. When I became a teacher, I vowed to make every student feel the way she made me feel. When I became a principal, I vowed to make every staff member feel the way she made me feel.

My second encounter with a ruthless teacher occurred when I was in seventh grade with Mrs. Eleanor Fryer. She was a native of Atlanta, a proud graduate of Spelman College, and a bona fide piece of work! Mrs. Fryer could "code-switch" like no other teacher I've ever known. You know that auntie who has all the trappings of class, culture, and sophistication in one setting, and when it's just family, and you get out of line, can switch it up and get "straight hood?" Well, that was Mrs. Fryer.

Her classroom was home, and we were both her students and grandchildren. Her style was completely different from Sr. Mary Claire's. Mrs. Fryer threw blackboard erasers with the precision of an NFL quarterback. She'd put you on blast, and could "signify" with the best of them. When she came upon two students arguing with escalating tension, hurling insults back and forth, often about each other's mamas, she'd step between them, roast (insult) both of them, then walk away amid cheers that would rival a Muhammad Ali seventh round knockout. The two students would retreat sheepishly to their respective corners, with wry smiles, and the nonsense would be shut down.

And don't worry about students who found themselves wearing four white chalk stripes across their backs from eraser missiles. It was a badge of honor to incur her wrath. I remember jumping back away from a thoughtful friend who tried to wipe the stripes from my shirt! I wore those stripes as if they were awarded for exemplary military service. Why? Because as hard-core as she was, I knew she loved us and demanded the best of us. There wasn't one malicious bone in her body.

It was like having your sassy, classy grandma teaching social studies.

One day, Mrs. Fryer asked to speak with me. She sat me down and seemingly out of nowhere shared the history of Morehouse College, its proud history, distinguished alumni, and its important place in history. I don't remember every detail of our one-way conversation, but I do remember her looking *through* me, and said with absolute certainty, "You're going to Morehouse College." That was it for me because four years later, I applied to one school: Morehouse College. After graduating high school, with barely two nickels to rub together and a "questionable" tuition check my dad wrote to buy my mother and him some time to scrape up funds, I made my way to Morehouse College.

Sister Mary Claire and Mrs. Fryer had one thing in common. They embodied the values of Ruthless Equity. None of the adversity my family endured ever calibrated their expectations. For them, my circumstances created urgency. Both of them were in touch with this Rule of Ruthlessness: *The Answers Are in the Room.*

They leaned into their skills, strengths, resources, and networks, which resulted in them leaning away from what they couldn't control regarding my background and circumstances. They looked past my family's financial challenges, my Wonder Bread-bag lunchbox, and sometimes hand-me-down clothes. They looked past the typical narrative about a Black boy from the hood. They saw more in me than I saw in myself and spoke greatness into me. They challenged me to *do* and challenged me to *become.* And because they were influencers in my life, I had a difficult time ever letting them down. Sometimes I learned things *for* them; before understanding "the why."

TWO IS TOO FEW

Well, that's it! The only two educators who made a life-changing difference in my life during my thirteen years of K-12 schooling. Conservatively, I've had more than one hundred educators throughout my K-12 experience. And while I'm grateful for the two I highlighted here, two educators out of one hundred are far too few. And I'm not an exception. I've surveyed tens of thousands of educators across North America. I ask, "How many can name one educator who made a life-altering positive impact in your life?" More than ninety percent of the audience of educators raise a hand. When I ask how many of can name two educators, it drops to about seventy-five percent. When I ask who had three educators who made this kind of impact, responses are well below thirty percent. Asking who can name four or more impactful educators brings a feeling of awkwardness to the space, coupled with the relaxing sound of crickets chirping.

There should've been more, and one of the goals of this book is to grow that number. Students spend most of their waking hours with educators, which provides you with the opportunity to become a significant influencer their lives.

MIRRORS AND WINDOWS

The goal of Complacency is to have you focus on what you can't control so much that you don't have the bandwidth to consider what you can and do control. Complacency seeks to have you stand at the window, look out, and point to factors that prevent you from being your best ruthless self. Complacency seeks to have you externalize every issue to the point of powerlessness.

Ruthless Equity places you in front of the mirror because the mirror reveals the source of your power. When you use windows just for sunlight and scenery, and stand firmly footed in front of the mirror, challenges become context for how you respond. When you synergize with colleagues, you become even more confident. Standing in the mirror isn't about *burden* or *blame*. It's about **power** and **control**.

You must operate understanding that *the answers are in the room*. The answers don't always appear instantly or come easily. Standing in the mirror requires an element of belief; belief in your own strengths, the strength of your team, staff, leaders, network, and resources.

As the guide on your side and the coach on your shoulder, I'm here to tell you that every time you produce results from the mirror, you are forever better as an educator. Your conviction grows, this process moves from mechanical to one you engage without thinking. It becomes part of your Ruthless Equity DNA.

THE RUTHLESS DON'T WONDER

From my first day as a teacher, my fundamental assumption was; "I am the difference for my students." That mindset didn't shield me from learning curves and making mistakes. And I wasn't great at teaching everything. I just assumed that being a teacher meant I had to find the keys to unlock learning for every student, regardless of background or circumstance. Almost 30 years later, consulting today with teachers and leaders, I feel the same way today as I did in August of 1992. How about you?

I DON'T WONDER IF I CAN MAKE A DIFFERENCE, I AM THE DIFFERENCE.

THE RUTHLESS DON'T CARE WHERE THE ANSWER COMES FROM

Your team meeting is about to begin. Megan, one of your teammates, enters the room and is clearly frustrated. She says, "I'm about to pull my hair out! I don't know what else to do! I've tried everything to reach Cole, but again and again, he's falling short and struggling!" She pulls the lining of her pants pockets out like rabbit ears, symbolizing she's got nothing else; she's out of ideas and strategies. What's the message *behind* Megan's frustration?

There are two possible scenarios:

Scenario 1: Megan is putting the team on notice that she's tried everything! Therefore, any suggestion of other strategies to try will be interpreted as an indictment of her teaching and taken personally. As a result, no one shares any strategies and instead showers her with warm reassurance that she did all she can, because, after all, Megan is the real victim here. In this scenario, Cole loses, Megan loses, and the team loses. The team soothes Megan without realizing how this enabling is just another form of Complacency.

Scenario 2: Megan's frustration is an open invitation for anyone to suggest additional ideas and solutions. Megan is casting a wide net, tapping into the collective genius of teammates in the service of ensuring learning for Cole. In this scenario, Cole wins, Megan wins, and the team wins.

Megan removed her ego, and focused on the mission-driven outcome. Ruthless educators don't care where the answer comes from; they just want to find the answer.

Which of these two scenarios is most aligned with your wiring, and why?

Scenario 1 or 2?_____

Explain your decision:

_____

_____

_____

If Scenario 1 is more aligned with how you work, then I honor your willingness to face an uncomfortable truth, and challenge you to take steps to release your ego and fully embrace learning as outcome. If your work aligns more with Scenario 2, then I challenge you to illuminate the way for others when situations provide an opportunity to do so. Remember, illuminating so that others see your model is an effective strategy for status-quo disruption and cultural change.

VISION, POVERTY, AND OPPORTUNITY

So many schools with a significant percentage of their students beneath the poverty line have a common thread of challenges plaguing their culture. It's tough enough for students who endure diminished access to housing, healthcare, and other basic needs. Prejudice regarding race, faith, and income are also major sources of stress and often interfere with healthy development and learning.

In a 2019 report, "From a Nation at Risk to a Nation at Hope," the National Commission on Social, Emotional, and Academic Development said, "These stressors are often compounded when low-income students and students of color also attend schools with fewer resources, more disruptions, lower expectations, and less-engaging learning experiences."

The commission goes further, asserting, "Providing equitable opportunities for developing young people socially, emotionally, and academically requires calibrating to each student's and school's individual strengths and needs while ensuring that those with greater needs have access to greater resources."

Here's our opportunity to be ruthless about re-culturing our schools in high-poverty communities. You can't impact every factor listed above, but you can target the factors within your sphere of influence; resource allocation, disruptions (scheduling), and engaging learning experiences.

With respect to resources, I'm not suggesting that a simple phone call will result in a truck dropping off tons of additional resources the next morning. I'm suggesting that schools identify priorities and then take a surgical look at what resources they have and where they are allocated. What creative opportunities do you see? Is every resource being allocated in ways that align with your school's mission? Before complaining about what you don't have, you should take full advantage of every resource at your disposal.

At my school, this process took place just after we clarified and committed to our shared mission and shared vision. Our shared mission was to ensure high levels of learning for all students, regardless of background. Our shared vision was for our school to compete with the high-performing schools in the area. Collectively, we painted a picture of what that would look like at our school. We identified the look, the feel, and most importantly, the behavioral collective commitments aligned with a high-performing school. Then we proceeded to hold that lens over every policy and practice at our school, and engage in tough conversations that encouraged us to make tough status-quo-disrupting decisions.

We did this with our master schedule as well. Because our mission was clear, we became ruthless about our schedule reflecting our priorities. It wasn't a simple process by any means, but it was easy to identify both alignment and misalignment. And because we kept our mission at the center of everything we did, it was never personal. Our changes reflected our shared mission rather than the individual mission of the leader.

In the book, *It's About Time*, authors Buffum and Mattos provide two universal truths we used to create an equity-focused master schedule.

1. Every student does not learn the same way: Every student has unique learning needs, based on his or her prior knowledge and experiences, cultural values, learning styles, and aptitudes. Due to these differences, no matter how well a teacher teaches a concept, we know some students won't get it the first time, because the best way to teach a concept to one student might fail miserably with another student in the same class.

2. Every student does not develop at the same speed: We know that there are spans of time in which students mature, both physically and intellectually. Some of these developmental spans, such as the period in which students start to show the physical changes of puberty, can be quite significant—it is not uncommon for a high school classroom to have a boy still waiting for his growth spurt sitting next to a fellow classmate who is a foot taller and already shaving. Less visible to the eye, but just as age-appropriate and extreme, are the differences in which adolescents develop intellectually and socially. Just as a group of boys won't develop the need to shave at the same speed or on the same day, secondary school students will not acquire the ability to solve abstract equations or display empathy at the same speed.

Many schools treat the existing master schedule like the Ten Commandment brought down from the mountain by Moses. As a result, they deem creating a schedule that provides protected time and support for teachers and students to learn and grow as an impossibility. But the fact is, while the schedule may present challenges in adjusting, the bottom line is, the master schedule is a reflection of your school's priorities. And I'm always amazed to see how human beings change, adjust, and manipulate time to meet needs deemed important or worthy. So, are your students worth it?

Our school was plagued with high rates of discipline referrals. Ours was a disruptive environment in total chaos. Suspension rates were through the roof, especially for an elementary school. There was a classroom designated for I.S.S. (in-school-suspension) that was so full so often, that it resembled a regular classroom of students. There were high levels of disrespect for teachers, which, in the dysfunctional climate I inherited, spilled over into many instances of disrespect going in both directions, from teachers to students.

It came as no surprise to me that "discipline" was at the top of the list of concerns for staff. They wanted to know what I, as the new principal was going to do about it. I made a deal with them. I told them that I would address discipline issues if they simultaneously addressed student engagement issues in the context of both instruction and classroom culture. I arranged professional development for staff around identified areas of need.

There were plenty of no-cost opportunities for us to be ruthless and get better. Our improvement efforts centered on these questions:

1. What are common characteristics of a high-performing school?
2. What is the look, sound, and feel of a high-performing school?
3. Would how we engage with our parents change if we were a high-performing school?
4. What would we expect of students at a high-performing school?

My goal is to provide a look inside our collective mind for some of the issues we considered, and how we became ruthless about transforming the narrative of our school.

COMPLACENCY AND DEMOGRAPHICS

You know the story: Your "*population*" has changed. This *demographic* is *different*. The change has caused an undercurrent of whispers of how it "used to be around here" and "what you once were able to get done," and now all that has changed, and the results bear it out. The prevailing perception is that your school has an increase of behaviors, less of a community feel, and a new "*element*," designated as "a priority school," or what I like to refer to as "that school." You're on a watch list and feeling even more pressure to "raise test scores."

In the midst of all hell breaking loose at your school, you attend professional development, where you learn of another school in your area making amazing breakthroughs. They're experiencing consistent success—and do you know what else? That school community shares some of the same characteristics yours has. The community has changed over time. They're more diverse than ever—and get this, they also serve a student population with a significant percentage of students who speak English as a second language. At that other school, the percentage of students receiving free and reduced lunch is even higher than at your school! Now you're frustrated and feeling like a failure. The message that you're at a "bad school" is coming across loud and clear.

More times than not, the above scenario doesn't end up offering an amazing opportunity to draft off the success of the other school. The typical reaction is often defensive and cloaked Complacency. Sometimes Complacency moves you to ask to see *more* examples like that school. In truth, you're not asking for more confirmation. You ask, hoping this example is so rare that their results can be deemed an aberration, and therefore not possible for your campus. You'll dig even more deeply into their data to find differences that diminish the comparison with your school.

Then come complaints about your school's lack of resources, lack of leadership, lack of parent engagement. Every hard question will move you further and further away from the other school's breakthroughs being a model for your school, and closer to the comfort of status-quo Complacency.

WHAT YOU FOCUS ON GROWS

TAKE UP ONE IDEA MAKE THAT ONE IDEA YOUR LIFE
THINK OF IT, DREAM OF IT, LIVE ON THAT IDEA.
LET THE BRAIN, MUSCLES, NERVES,
EVERY PART OF YOUR BODY BE FULL OF THAT IDEA,
AND JUST LEAVE EVERY OTHER IDEA ALONE.
THIS IS THE WAY TO SUCCESS,
THIS IS THE WAY GREAT SPIRITUAL GIANTS ARE PRODUCED.
—VIVEKANANDA

ALL STUDENTS GROW BY USING THEIR STRENGTHS

ALL human beings grow by leveraging their strengths. The most effective way to improve underdeveloped skills is to use your strengths. Think about the day you interviewed for your current position. You walked into the office or conference room, and sitting there was either the principal and/or a panel of leaders ready to interview you. It's time for you to sell yourself by highlighting your strengths. But imagine for a moment answering this way: "Before I share the experiences and qualities that make me a great fit for your school, please allow me begin with a detailed breakdown of my weakest areas as an educator." Sounds ridiculous, right?

Teachers must mine for the strengths that exist within every student and work with those strengths and gifts to improve students' underdeveloped skills. An internet search will reveal *elevendy-hundred* different inventories, tools, and questions to help you discover students' gifts.

With a team of colleagues, discuss the powerful questions offered by Howard Pitler, Associate Professor at Emporia State University in his blog;

The Six Questions to Ask Your Students on Day One:
You're invited to step into the shoes of your students by answering these questions for yourself.

1. What are you passionate about?

2. How do you want to be recognized?

3. What do you see as your greatest strength?

4. What name do you want used when calling on you in class?

5. What will a successful school year look and feel like at the end of the year?

6. What are the characteristics or attributes you want in a teacher?

Complacency hopes you begin the year by leaning more into marginalizing labels than on your strengths as a teacher, and the strengths of every student. You've got to be intentional about discovering strengths, and leveraging them to ensure high levels of learning.

CLASS ROSTERS: SET UP FOR FAILURE

PEOPLE AREN'T BORN SMART, THEY BECOME SMART.
—DR. JEFF HOWARD, FOUNDER, THE EFFICACY INSTITUTE

Here's my sense of the plight of classroom teachers at the start of each school year: Class rosters are distributed with student names along with the fifteen things wrong with each student. This may sound like an exaggeration, but is it really? Teachers start the year pummeled by direct that work in favor of the "bell-shaped curse" and against a culture of equity for all.

Class rosters are not constructed with the intent to place doubt in the minds of teachers or limit the opportunities for some students. But the reality is, rosters often result in both unintended outcomes. The initial intention of labeling; to organize and target resources, devolves into diminished expectations and marginalized students.

Pretty quickly, notions of flexible grouping based on warm real-time data devolves into ability grouping based on cold aggregate data from the past, and limiting perceptions of the present. You've got to stay the course and start with student strengths in the service of equity for all.

Keri Hughes is a 2nd grade teacher at Clear Creek Elementary in Cartersville, Georgia. She shares a great example of Ruthless Equity involving a student who by age 7 had a well-earned reputation that resulted in negative adult perceptions and low expectations for learning.

"Our mission was to grow a group of students performing below grade-level in reading to of grade level or better, by identifying the essential standards each student had yet to master. We then matched like needs into groups and worked for an hour every afternoon. Troy is a very challenging student. He is known to have both significant behavioral and learning challenges. Admittedly, teaching Troy is exhausting at times. Because of this, I was intentional about connecting with him relationally, and got to work."

"The time came to check-in and assess his progress. I assessed him on two the standards and he *slayed* the assessment, demonstrating proficiency for each standard! When I shared his data along with the paperwork to move him to proficient levels of performance, his assessment results were met with doubt. Another staff member decided to assess him again, and concluded that he was not proficient. I was told "he's not proficient" and "he's not capable.""

"These two remarks confirmed to me that some were insinuating that I fudged the results. Granted, his assessment results were better with me than with the staff member. So, a day later, I invited Troy back to my room. I didn't want to make this about me or my ego, so, I asked another teacher, who had no knowledge of the situation to assess him. I said, "Troy, you did this for me yesterday, and now she wants to see how smart you are. Can you do it again?" He smiled at me, got to work, and scored one-hundred percent on the assessment."

"When students know we expect nothing from them, they will give nothing. I'm not a super teacher. I didn't do anything magical. I just didn't let adult perceptions and his avoidance behaviors excuse him from learning essential standards."

ALLERGIES, CUSTODY, AND TABULA RASA

When I began my teaching career, I thought I was ready for everything. What I wasn't prepared for was what lay inside the student cumulative folder. This folder followed students from grade-level to grade-level and from school to school. The folder was full of information teachers were required to update throughout the school year. It contained data, student work samples, assessments, conclusions, artifacts, meeting notes, and concerns.

I remember opening the first folder and then shutting it after reading for just three minutes. There were references to learning delays, a lack of motivation, and low ability to learn. I hadn't met this student yet, and already my brain was forming conclusions and calibrating expectations. I was making judgments. I didn't like the way I felt. I made a decision that day to not read any more of them. But when I learned that the cumulative file could also contain important information, about medical and custody issues, I could no longer completely ignore the folder. As a compromise, I learned how to identify the forms with medical and custody info, and simply scan each folder for that information. I sought information about two things when I opened a folder: allergies and custody.

After all, I had plans for a mock economy in my classroom, and if someone was allergic to peanuts, there will be no Snicker bars available for purchase from PosseMart (we were The Posse, and PosseMart was our Fun Friday store). And, if there was a custody concern, I needed to know that as well.

Beyond those two issues, I read nothing else because I didn't want any labels messing with my expectations. I proceeded with the mantra, *What I need to know about my students will find me.* This approach served me then as a classroom teacher, and now as a trainer, consultant, and coach.

I am not endorsing this as recommended practice. I know how important cumulative folder information is. I'm suggesting that you figure out the best metacognitive path to what I call a "tabula rasa mindset." In Latin, *tabula rasa* means "clean slate." In my classroom, every student had a clean slate. Find your own path to preventing information from placing a ceiling on your expectations of your students, and limits on what you can accomplish as a teacher.

How will/do you create the "tabula rasa" conditions that provide every student with a "clean slate?"

_____

_____

_____

LABELS ARE FINE UNTIL THEY DIMINISH YOUR EXPECTATIONS.

RUTHLESS RELATIONSHIPS AND RIGOR

Does every student you serve know you're glad they showed up? How are you intentional about making your learning space a welcoming place that fosters belonging and inclusion? How do you connect with your students? Addressing these questions helps to lay a foundation for fruitful relationships.

Some educators cultivate positive relationships with students, but don't challenge students to achieve academically. They don't take advantage of relational capital and become warm demanders. These educators develop relationships with students for reasons other than advancing school's fundamental purpose, ensuring learning. Whether it's done for approval rating, or because the teacher is a people-pleaser, when relational capital isn't invested in advancing learning, it's a wasted opportunity.

It was 2:45 p.m. on a Wednesday afternoon during my first year as a teacher. There were small-group conversations happening all over the school library as we waited for the 3:00 pm staff meeting to begin. I sat within earshot of our music teacher and physical education teacher. I couldn't make out exactly what they were saying, but I knew it was juicy! I slyly leaned forward in my chair to eavesdrop without intruding. They were going on and on about the rowdy behavior of a specific class. I was going through my Rolodex of teacher names, positing guesses on who led this rowdy and unruly classroom.

My interest was piqued. I put my pride aside, and said, "OMG, I couldn't help overhearing your conversation! Whose class are you talking about?" There are moments in life when a three-second pause feels like three hours. The two of them looked startled and awkward. The music teacher finally spoke and said, "your class." I said a silent prayer hoping to spontaneously combust in that moment.

I had what I'd call a *spirited* class that year. While I don't parse every word in cumulative folders, sometimes a class of students earns and/or gets saddled with a negative reputation. So, while thinking of my class as *bad* wasn't aligned with my wiring, I referred to them as *spirited*. The behaviors they described were ones I hadn't seen since the first couple of weeks of school. I worked hard to cultivate relationships, embed incentives, provide high levels of engagement, and opportunities for authentic encouragement. In talking with my colleagues, I realized that while my intention was to create a productive learning environment, that wasn't my only objective. My ego wanted to show and prove to my colleagues that *these* students could and would behave appropriately for *me*. While accomplishing that goal, I failed to provide students with *why* that mattered. I communicated a *why* that served my ego and not their growth. I was not their only teacher that year, and while they conducted themselves appropriately with me, they didn't carry those same expectations to other learning spaces. My pursuit of *cool* resulted in me failing them, and I had to devote precious time and energy helping them unlearn and relearn the how and why of appropriate behavior in all learning settings. From that moment on, I became consumed with keeping the fundamental purpose of my work as an educator at the center of everything I did, thought, decided, and acted upon. I wasn't perfect moving forward, but installing that filter helped me get back to center quickly whenever I found myself straying off course.

When it comes to building relationships, they should never be cultivated in isolation or for your ego. Ruthless educators regard relationships as a requirement to become an influencer in the service of ensuring learning. As humans, we learn from people we like and respect. We learn best from people who see us and make us feel like we belong. The influencers in your life challenge you, stretch you, and demand your best from you. Every day offers a fresh opportunity for you to be *that* influencer in *their* lives.

DON'T PROJECT BROKENNESS ONTO YOUR STUDENTS

The global pandemic was upon us, causing upheaval, disruption, and uncertainty in schools. There was a lot of worry and hand-wringing going on during the weeks leading up to schools' opening. Teachers far and wide fretted about how broken students would be during those first weeks in class. Hearts were in the right place, and I understood the root of their worry.

For many teachers, this worry led to plans to "put-aside academics" in the service of focusing solely on students' social and emotional needs. This stance was supported far and wide on social media platforms, and I became concerned; not with the intent, but with the assumptions. Understanding that there was no "pandemic playbook" to guide us, I can see how many came to conclude that students will return to school traumatized, but the fact is, there was no evidence of this. There was no evidence because students had not returned to school.

The best way to gauge the impact of the pandemic, or any challenging condition, is to engage students in learning, and be ready to respond and support evidence of issues that impede learning for students. Assuming any student will be broken and not ready to engage in learning, is a slippery slope of judgment. The application of any intervention, including SEL (social-emotional learning), should be based on an issue impeding the learning for a student. You can't know that until you engage the student in instruction.

The "well-intentioned" part of this issue might make you question if it's a form of Complacency. But don't be fooled. This is *definitely* Complacency, subtle in appearance and potent in its impact. It is Complacency dipped in essential oils intent on relaxing your senses.

The only thing I hear being talked about regarding SEL is the S(ocial) and E(motional) part of the term. Complacency has educators leaving off the L(earning) part of SEL. These discussions take place on platforms that often-become groupthink echo chambers, and the students directly affected are almost always the ones who can least afford it. Please don't project brokenness onto your students.

Don't Project Brokenness Onto Your Students

Guiding Question: How do you respond when you hear statements that cast your students as *broken*?

THESE THREE THINGS

Three things all Ruthless Equity educators have in common.

They:

1. Assume nothing.
2. Prepare for everything.
3. Respond based on evidence.

Let evidence of student learning inform your next steps; not perceptions, opinions, or assumptions.

BOXES CHECKED ON BOTH SIDES

> I LIVE FOR SPEAKING LIFE INTO CHILDREN. WE MUST INDEED GIVE THEM A REPUTATION TO LIVE UP TO. TELL THEM THEY ARE LEADERS, BRILLIANT, AND SMART. PLANT AND WATER THE SEEDS INSIDE THEM.
> —CARLENE JOHNSON-STEELE, GRADE-FIVE SUPERVISOR, ST. MARY, JAMAICA

Early in my teaching career, I read an article by Carol Ann Tomlinson, a preeminent leader in curriculum design and differentiated instruction. In this article, she shared her experience with taking the "gifted curriculum" and using it with her "regular education" students. Her action research yielded positive results and reinforced the power of teacher expectations and the self-fulfilling prophecy. It shaped my mindset as an educator and influenced my work with students then and with teachers and leaders now.

Tomlinson's work helped to shape the following belief: If all the characteristics of a student with special needs were listed down the left side of the page, and all the characteristics of giftedness were listed down the right side, every single one of us would have boxes checked on both sides. From that day forward, I have treated every learner as both gifted and special needs.

Boxes Checked On Both Sides

Guiding Question: How will you discover the gifts and strengths of every one of your students?

OPPORTUNITY VS. ENSURE

There's a difference between providing students with the *opportunity* to learn and *ensuring* they learn. For essential learning outcomes, the only outcome is to ensure learning, even when students want to opt-out of the process. For non-essential learning outcomes, providing the opportunity to master those outcomes is acceptable. Some students will master non-essential content and some won't. Once upon a time in our schools, providing students the opportunity to learn was norm. This norm is no more. So, stay in tune with your language and the actions that follow. For essentials, your mission is to ensure learning (you're on the hook), and not simply provide students the opportunity to learn (you're off the hook).

THE DIFFERENCE BETWEEN IMPORTANT AND ESSENTIAL

I like my arms. They're important and useful. I'd like to keep them for the remainder of my life. However, if I lost an arm in an accident, and received medical attention in a timely manner, it's reasonable to conclude that I could continue to live a productive life. My arm is **important**.

I also like my heart. It's very useful. But if it stops beating, you can, in the words of the great comedian Richard Pryor, *cancel Christmas*. I can't live without my heart because it's **essential**. It's important to distinguish between important learning outcomes and essential learning outcomes.

RUTHLESS EQUITY IS NOT STUDENT-BACKGROUND-DEPENDENT

Who is the student who makes you consider stashing a full flask of bourbon in the drawer of your desk? The student whose first name made you shudder when you heard a stranger say it while on vacation? The student who moved you to go to Barnes & Noble with a black Sharpie intent on crossing out that name in every "baby name book" the store carries? Who is that student? Write his/her name below. Do it! You can't start healing until you write it out loud.

Who is "that student" for you? _____

Who is the teacher known for getting results from students with the worst track record and reputation? The teacher everyone knows for connecting with the worst-behaved, most apathetic, most disruptive, and most disengaged students? You may have chalked it up to luck the first time you saw her do it, but after a few years, you acknowledge that her success isn't about luck, even if you can't fully explain how she gets it done. When you look at the student you named, you know deep down this educator would find a way, don't you? Yes, you do.

Complete the prompt:

I know my colleague _____ would find a way to reach and connect with _____.

WHAT DOES S(HE) DO THAT I CAN ADD TO MY TOOLBOX?

RUTHLESS REMINDERS

- Depend more on the collective genius of staff, not the factors outside your control.
- Three things all Ruthless Equity educators have in common.
- They:
    1. Assume nothing.
    2. Prepare for everything.
    3. Respond based on evidence.

- You build relationships with students to impact their learning.
- What you focus on, grows.
- Ruthless Equity is not student background-dependent.
- Take a *tabula rasa* approach with your students.
- Don't project brokenness onto your students.

DISRUPTIVE ACTION TO TAKE

With a team of colleagues, discuss the following questions:

....

....

....

Which topic in this chapter most strongly affirmed your current thinking and practice? Explain why.

....

....

....

Which topic in this chapter most challenged your current thinking and practice? Explain why.

....

....

....

What do you commit to do differently as a result of your reflection?

....

....

....

CHAPTER SEVEN

THE THIRD RULE OF RUTHLESSNESS
A COMMITMENT TO:
START WITH THE CROWN

DON'T GET CUTE

Equitable practice begins with identifying grade-level essential learning outcomes in every course and content area. Do you see any mention of exceptions? Any, "except for..." or "unless of course your school is located in..." or "the exception is if the demographic of your school is..." or "districts that think a lot of themselves can just skip this?" You don't see any exceptions, because there are none. *And yet, so many districts fall prey to a special edition of Complacency: they get cute.* They start chipping away at the rules of engagement. When I consult with schools, here are the two examples of creating exceptions:

- Low-achieving schools change conditions because they believe their challenges are the exception. Staff suffers from collective low self-esteem. As a result, they won't commit to equitable practice because they don't believe they'll work with their student population/demographic. They don't believe things can change.
- High-performing schools with inflated staff esteem wonder why they need to change anything. In some cases, they brag about the number of "touchdowns" they score, while being located in communities where most of their students are born on the "two-yard line." They dislike being asked to change.

As a result of Complacency's double-barreled assault, both schools take implementation liberties that sabotage their efforts. They ensure learning for some, but not for all. Equity cannot exist without essential outcomes. As a reminder, essential learning outcomes are the knowledge, skills, and dispositions in every course and content area that every student must master to be successful at:

- the next grade-level
- the next course
- the high-stakes assessment (where applicable), and
- life beyond the K-12 school system

There is no "substitute for" or "working around" essential outcomes. Your district changing the terminology doesn't change this fact. I don't care how you dress it up, or what you spray it with, if equity is your outcome, then identifying essential learning outcomes is necessary. Stop trying to cut corners. Stop running. Make a commitment and **do the work** equity calls us to do.

FORTY YEARS

Your Grumpy Uncle is back!

I'm at a point where I just smile and nod my head when I hear educators go on about how *hot* a topic equity is today; as if equity has been held in captivity and found some way to escape. The number of requests I've gotten from schools and districts that want to address equity is awesome, but (and this is a big butt):

THE PLC AT WORK PROCESS IS, AND HAS ALWAYS BEEN AN EQUITY INITIATIVE. PLCS HAVE BEEN ADDRESSING EQUITY FOR MORE THAN FORTY YEARS.

Take a moment and come outside with me, past my patio and off my back porch where I'm grilling. Your Grumpy Uncle needs to speak to you like family for a moment: "Listen, *equity ain't nuthin new.* You may be noticing it more than ever, and, that's a good thing! In fact, we seasoned equity warriors are glad you're here because *we've been waiting.* But the work of equity has been here. It's getting more attention than ever, but it's not new. I'm proud to say equity has been at the center of my work for thirty years, and those of us who've been here are going to make sure equity remains rooted in culture, mindset, practice and improved student learning results!"

In a professional learning community or PLC, there are four critical questions that guide the cycle of teaching, learning, and assessment:

1. **What do we expect every student to know and be able to do?**
2. How will we know when students have learned it?
3. How will we respond when students haven't learned it?
4. How will we respond when students already know it?

Question 1 is in **bold** print for a reason. After you establish a culture of belonging and inclusion, this is where the instructional part of equity begins. Question 1 asks you to identify essential learning outcomes; and monitoring every student's progress toward mastery of every essential outcome is the work. Providing the support, resources, and time for students to master essential learning outcomes is where the cycle ends, and then you begin the process again with a new set of essential outcomes. Without identifying essential learning outcomes, you are not a PLC, and you cannot pursue equity. Period. No exceptions.

How to "fit in" PLCs

Guiding Question: Do PLCs feel like yet another *initiative* at your school?

START WITH THE CROWN, NOT WITH THE KID

ABOVE THE HEAD OF EVERY STUDENT, MOREHOUSE HOLDS A CROWN SHE CHALLENGES THEM TO GROW TALL ENOUGH TO WEAR. —DR. HOWARD THURMAN, '23 EDUCATOR, MINISTER, THEOLOGIAN, PHILOSOPHER, AND AUTHOR

Dr. Thurman's quote was on the back cover of the Morehouse College brochure I received in 1984 as a high school junior. That quote was seared into my soul upon reading it, as it defined my approach as a classroom teacher, a school leader, and today, as an author, speaker, and consultant.

When I refer to *starting with the crown, the crown* represents the essential learning outcomes every student must master. The crown identifies that place where all students must go in a particular content area. Teachers hold the crown above the head of their students and grow each student tall enough to wear the crown. Some students will grow *to* the crown, other will grow *through* the crown, but we cannot settle for students falling short of wearing the crown.

Teachers operating under Complacency's hold don't start with the *crown*, they start with the *kid*. They shoulder the heavy burden of judgment; deciding "who can" and "who can't" learn. So, instead of one crown (equity), each student has a crown that is held at various heights based on teacher judgement. This form of Complacency opens the way for bias, inequity, and widening performance gaps.

A guaranteed and viable curriculum isn't a platitude. It means to guarantee mastery for all essential learning outcomes. Guaranteed means just that—guaranteed! You do whatever it takes to ensure mastery of these targets. Viable is another way of saying, "less is more." It's impossible to guarantee mastery learning of every target in every course or content area. There are just too many to consider. Viable means a reasonable number of targets students must master. The "whatever it takes" approach applies to the targets you have to guarantee all students master, the essential learning outcomes.

When you *Start With The Crown*, it removes *judgment* from the equation. It removes the pressure to judge who can and who can't learn. Essential means essential. Students must master the outcome. When you understand that, you remove questions about whether students can or cannot learn. These questions are moot. You must set about the mission of ensuring mastery learning for every student. When you remove "can they?" or "can't they?" from the equation, you open the way for maximum levels of creativity, resourcefulness, problem-solving, innovation, and collaboration.

You put your back to the wall, face the challenges that come with learning, and focus on the outcome of growing every student "to and through The Crown." Remember, regarding The Crown, addressing one question and one question only: *How will we get every student there?* This makes the work of equity simple to understand (and not easy to do):

1. Identify The CROWN (essential learning outcomes).
2. Treat essential learning outcomes like they're *essential* for every student to master.
3. Monitor every student's progress toward mastery of essential learning outcomes (grow students To and Through The CROWN).

MISSION KICKS IN WHEN THE MATH STOPS WORKING

Recall a time when you were on a mission to make something happen with logic and odds stacked against you. Not a life-or-death situation, just one you treated with life-or-death urgency. The odds were not in your favor. People around you explained that it was next to impossible. Logically, you had little to no chance of making it happen. Nothing was adding up because *the math stopped working*.

However, success was the *only* option for you. This is when you become mission-driven and turn the obstacles standing in your path into the context for your response. Recall the earlier example when a *mother* morphs into a *mutha*. This is what happens when we decide to make mission happen.

MISSION KICKS IN WHEN THE MATH STOPS WORKING.

You unleashed a focused and urgent energy in the service of making your desired outcome happen. And while this formula is no guarantee of success, I bet you'd look back and conclude that you made the seemingly impossible happen more times than not. That's because when we unleash this type of urgent focus, we are apt to be at our best. The obstacles in your path cease to be excuses and are now context for your response; mere pawns on your chessboard to be removed.

THE 3 C'S OF URGENCY IN A PLC

1. **Clarity:** Remember Question One of a PLC: *What do we expect every student to learn?* **Clarity** is the answer. When seeking clarity on how to approach your goals, ask yourself this: What are the agreed-upon essential skills and competencies every student must master to be successful at the next grade-level, the next course, the high-stake assessment, and life beyond the K-12 system?

2. **Conviction:** Identifying essential learning outcomes is a huge step, and it must be coupled with an unwavering **conviction** to ensure every student masters those outcomes. You place your back to the wall, and the only way out is the door named *Mastery*. You communicate to both students and parents that mastery is the only option for outcomes identified as essential.

3. **Constraints:** Think back on a personal goal you've had. The likelihood of achieving the goal increased when you applied a time **constraint** to the goal. Ensuring mastery of essential learning outcomes operates the same way.

When you add these three elements to your work, it will draw your attention to other aspects of collaboration. Team norms become important because you want to maximize the time you meet as a team. Data analysis goes from simply identifying which students *got it* and which ones *didn't* to becoming a tool to inform instruction, intervention, and acceleration. When you don't have these elements of urgency embedded in your work, you're operating in a passive state.

COMPLACENCY'S B.U.R.P.

Why do we struggle so much with ensuring equity? Like *growth mindset*, we sing its praises as a theory, we highlight it in social media posts, we're motivated by speakers who emphasize equity, and discuss it during book studies. We wear T-shirts, buy posters, and quote passages. We are *all-in* up to the moment the work moves from *platitude* to *practice*, from *idea* to *instruction*.

There are four major forms of Complacency that have us mentally shackled; **Complacency's B.U.R.P.:**

B—The **B**ell-Shaped Curse (Curve): Decades after the bell-shaped curve was debunked, we are still slaves to the notion that in a room of ten random students, there are going to be 2VS's, 6SS's and 2KD's...

Two *very smart* students
Six *sort of smart* students
Two *kind of dumb* students

U—Because behaviors follow beliefs, we create the conditions for numbers to fall out this way. And when they do, our archaic and damaging beliefs are reinforced. **U**nder (anything...): *under*served...*under*privileged...has us focused more on enabling students with charity, diminished expectations, pity, and less focused on coaching them up, advocating, empowering, accelerating, and forming high-expectations that lead to grade-level or better performance.

R—**R**anking, Sorting, and Selecting: Complacency has us devoting more energy to rewarding "first and fastest," ranking and sorting while moving us away from our fundamental and sacred purpose, which is to ensure **learning for all**.

P—**P**otential: When we calibrate expectations based on perceptions of student potential, we destroy the possibility of equitable practice. Complacency has somehow twisted our talk of determining student potential into something that sounds positive! We'll dig into this issue more soon!

Educators have helped to make Carol Dweck's groundbreaking book, *Mindset,* a well-deserved best seller. We love the idea of growth mindset so much, we're in the front row at her conferences, finishing her sentences as she speaks! And yet we're still rejecting the growth mindset in practice. Instead of adding enrichment opportunities, we continue to add more low groups. We develop new sophisticated vocabulary for our deficit models, clinging tightly to fixed mindset in so much of what we do.

GRADE-LEVEL OR BETTER

Question: Where do you predict a student will finish the year when taught below grade level all year long? I'll wait for your answer. Yes, they finish below grade-level. To achieve equity, all students must receive grade-level core instruction. Notice how I used the word *receive* *(all students must receive grade-level core instruction)*, and not *exposed* *(all student must be exposed to grade-level core instruction)*.

"Exposing students" to grade-level instruction has become a euphemism for another form of Complacency. Teachers "expose students" to appease decisions that support equity. Every time I hear the word *exposing* used in this context, I picture a student being "propped up" at a desk and made to look like he's a part of the class. As long as he stays propped up for the duration of the lesson, the objective of exposing him has been accomplished.

If you feel a headache coming on thinking about the idea of all students receiving grade-level core instruction, you're still grappling with your love of how growth mindset *sounds*, while unwilling to embed growth mindset into your practice. There must be protected time in the master schedule to provide some students with both acceleration and enrichment opportunities, and *all* students must receive instruction (with support) at grade-level or better. Remember, the outcome of *exposing* students to grade-level core instruction is *exposure*. The outcome of students *receiving* grade-level instruction is mastery *learning*.

HIGH-PERFORMING IN SPIRIT TODAY, AND RESULTS TOMORROW

For the past fifteen years, my *students* have been adult educators. Every audience represented a wide range of skills, experience, and knowledge. Without exception, my adult learners receive grade-level or better instruction, and they expect nothing less of me. They expect me to teach, coach, and train at the highest level of the standard and scaffold as appropriate. By scaffold, I'm referring to building learning supports as a bridge between where they are currently performing and the essential learning outcome (or better). I have essential learning outcomes for each audience, and ways to monitor and track mastery. Dr. Gloria Brodie is a great model for this principle of adult learning. I'll share how she embodies both the mindset and practice to embed Ruthless Equity on her campus.

Dr. Gloria Bodie is the principal of Moore Elementary School in Griffin, Georgia. I'm supporting every school in their district with the outcome of empowering teachers and leaders to embed equitable practices school-wide. They're building staff and district capacity to create a high-performing professional learning community at each school. Led by visionary superintendent Keith L. Simmons, Griffin-Spalding is in a school district committed to changing their narrative. Moore Elementary School represents a microcosm of districtwide challenges. Ninety percent of their students are eligible for free and reduced lunch benefits. They serve many families living in poverty. Currently, they rank in the bottom fifty percent in academic achievement in the state. Moore Elementary comes complete with a list of excuses to justify why students can't achieve at high levels. But you wouldn't know this when working with Dr. Brodie and her staff. I teach, coach, and train at the highest level of the standard, and Moore Elementary has responded in kind. I'm highlighting Dr. Brodie's leadership for two reasons:

1. **Visionary Mindset** — Dr. Brodie understands the power of visioning. With all the challenges staff faces on a daily basis, she understands the need to paint a compelling picture of the ideal future of their school. A compelling picture that inspires, clarifies aspirations, and identifies collective commitments. These three elements open the way for staff to *see past their current circumstances* and set their gaze on the school they seek to become. When you talk with Dr. Brodie, you hear this. She communicates like a leader of a high-performing school. And the process doesn't end here. They take action around the **right work**.

2. **A Willingness To Submit To Coaching/Taking Action—** My work with schools revolves around universal practice. By research-based practices that are effective at any school, regardless of performance level or demographics. Universal practice *works if you work it!* One of the challenges of school improvement work is when staff convince themselves that

they have *unique* circumstances that prevent recommended practice from being effective. I've worked with many schools with similar challenges to that of Moore, and when it's time to take action and engage in new practices, too often, it triggers resistance. The maddening irony is: the excuses offered for why they believe practices won't work are the very issues the practices are built to overcome. During one of our coaching sessions, I shared a data meeting protocol that many effective schools use to improve student learning results. The protocol streamlines the professional learning communities' process, provides clarity, support, and autonomy to collaborative teams, and allows school leaders to both monitor the process and support teachers without the burden of ineffective *snoopervision*. My check-in with Dr. Brodie revealed that she and her staff ran with it. They didn't "get cute" and alter the protocol based on perceptions, poverty, bias, circumstances, or assumptions. The school-wide structures and support she provided to every grade-level team, and the commitment to work through the learning curves associated with any new practice guarantees that Moore Elementary will become an achievement lighthouse in the Griffin-Spalding School District, state, and eventually, the nation. Dr. Gloria Brodie and the team at Moore Elementary School is high-performing in *spirit* today, and in *results* tomorrow.

TEACH TO THE HIGHEST LEVEL OF EVERY STANDARD

Teaching to the highest level of every standard has multiple benefits:

- This practice "speaks vision into the lives of students."
- Your once-marginalized students will be more confident, stronger, and smarter because of your combination of high-expectations with supports.

- Students demonstrating proficiency will have their learning extended and enriched.
- The gap between where students are and where they need to be will narrow because resources and support are targeted, informed by evidence, and aspirational as they move students to grade-level or better performance.

For some students who, over time, have been convinced they're low, slow, or dumb, you'll have to simply "know better for them" in the short term, until your support and their improved results changes their beliefs. Immerse them in an environment of enrichment; where mastery learning (with support) is the expectation. Let their resistance or excuses be an indicator that you need to persist with this paradigm shift, not an indicator that it's time to acquiesce and revert to old tired archaic practices.

In her book, *The Pedagogy of Confidence,* Dr. Yvette Jackson cites the three unequivocal beliefs reflective of Feuerstein's theory of Structural Cognitive Modification[2]:

1. Intelligence is modifiable.
2. All students benefit from a focus on high intellectual performance.
3. Learning is influenced by the interaction of culture, language, and cognition (National Urban Alliance, 2001).

George Couros, author of *The Innovator's Mindset*, asserts that teaching to the highest level of the standard and scaffolding as appropriate begins with one question, "What is best for *this* learner?" The answer to his question must be in the context of moving students To and Through The CROWN. The outcome for every student is to learn at grade-level or better. Couros' question asks us to figure out what each student needs to achieve the outcome.

Plan At The Highest Level Of Every Standard

Guiding Question: How soon will you apply this principle? In what content area?

LOUDER AND SLOWER

> ## NO PROBLEM CAN BE SOLVED FROM THE SAME LEVEL OF CONSCIOUSNESS THAT CREATED IT.
> ## — ALBERT EINSTEIN

When your team's analysis of common formative assessment data reveals that some students require extra time and support to master outcomes, it's important to remember:

> ## LOUDER AND SLOWER IS NOT RETEACHING.
> ## — DR. RICK DUFOUR

Reteaching students using the same instructional practices and strategies that didn't work the first time is likely not going to be effective the second time around. This underscores the power and the *why* of collaboration! When you've taught the content the best way you know how, and students don't "get it," it's an indicator to tap into the collective expertise of your collaborative team. When teams collaborate effectively, it serves as an instant, real-time professional learning opportunity. If your team can't provide a solution, then you widen your net to include action research, additional resources, the rest of your staff, colleagues throughout the district, and your online professional learning network. When you widen your circle of influence this way, with urgency, you aren't just *doing* equity, you're *living* equity.

MASTER TEACHER COMPETENCIES

With a team of colleagues, participate in the following activity.

Teammates should have some familiarity with one another, and work in pairs.

Directions:

1. Write your colleague's name in the space provided below.
2. Quietly, reflectively, and privately, read each master teacher competency and evaluate your partner's **highest individual potential** for mastering each competency.
3. Indicate your evaluation of their highest individual potential on the Likert scale located beneath each competency.
4. Evaluators are not permitted to select 7's in every area.
5. Invite partners to share their evaluations with each other.

Master Teacher Competencies

Colleague Name_____

1. Master educators are dedicated to making knowledge accessible to all students. They act on the belief that all students can learn.

Circle one of the following:

Never   1   2   3   4   5   6   7   Always

2. Master educators understand how students develop and learn. They incorporate the prevailing theories of cognition and intelligence in their practice.

Circle one of the following:

Never   1   2   3   4   5   6   7   Always

3. Master educators have a rich understanding of the subject(s) they teach and appreciate how knowledge in their subject is created, organized, linked to other disciplines, and applied to real-world settings.

Circle one of the following:

Never   1   2   3   4   5   6   7   Always

4. Master educators command specialized knowledge of how to convey and reveal subject matter to students. They are aware of the preconceptions and background knowledge that students typically bring to each subject, and of strategies and instructional materials that can be of assistance.

Circle one of the following:

Never   1   2   3   4   5   6   7   Always

5. Master educators create, enrich, maintain, and alter instructional settings to capture and sustain the interest of their students and to make the most effective use of time.

Circle one of the following:

Never   1   2   3   4   5   6   7   Always

6. Master educators can assess the progress of individual students as well as that of the class as a whole. They employ multiple methods for measuring student growth and understanding, and can clearly explain student performance to parents.

Circle one of the following:

Never   1 2 3 4 5 6 7   Always

7. Master educators are models of educated persons, exemplifying the virtues they seek to inspire in students—curiosity, honesty, fairness, respect for diversity, and appreciation of cultural differences.

Circle one of the following:

Never   1 2 3 4 5 6 7   Always

8. Master educators ensure students have the ability to reason and take multiple perspectives when being creative and taking risks, and to adopt an experimental and a problem-solving orientation.

Circle one of the following:

Never   1 2 3 4 5 6 7   Always

9. Master educators contribute to the effectiveness of the school by working collaboratively with other professionals on instructional policy, curriculum development, and staff development.

Circle one of the following:

Never   1 2 3 4 5 6 7   Always

10. Master educators find ways to work collaboratively and creatively with parents, engaging them productively in the work of the school.

Circle one of the following:

Never   1   2   3   4   5   6   7   Always

At the completion of this activity, respond to the reflection questions.

Use the space below and share your reflections about the activity. Discuss your reflections as a group.

How did rating your colleague's highest individual potential feel to you?

....

....

....

How did engaging this activity affect your thinking about determining the highest individual potential of your students?

....

....

....

THE LOW EXPECTATIONS OF HIGHEST INDIVIDUAL POTENTIAL

If you navigated that activity as directed, you're really glad it's over, aren't you? I'm not there with you and I know it was awkward as hell. I'm sure that few if any pairs evaluated all ten competencies, and wouldn't be surprised if some partners couldn't move beyond the awkwardness. Does it feel like I'm inside your head right now? Here's what I hope you learned from this experience:

EVALUATING THE HIGHEST INDIVIDUAL POTENTIAL OF MY COLLEAGUE IS NONE OF MY BUSINESS.

Now broaden the application of this conclusion. Ready for it?

EVALUATING THE HIGHEST INDIVIDUAL POTENTIAL OF MY STUDENTS IS NONE OF MY BUSINESS.

Yes, the same applies to your students. Sit with that for a moment. I know it's messing with you because we've gotten to a place where helping students reach their "highest individual potential" is regarded as a positive thing, and, dare I say it, a visionary aspiration. Canadian school leader and consultant Francois Masse shared this thought about H.I.P. (highest individual potential) in his work with schools: "When working with schools I often hear this statement: developing every child's potential. What does that mean? Though the intention may seem sincere, the fact is the statement hides the fact that teachers are applying different crowns to different kids. Does that give us permission to lower the crown for certain students because they do not have the potential? As if some students come to school with four cubes of potential, others with ten and some with one? This results in educators discriminating from the onset and institutionalizing gaps in learning!"

Are you still wondering if Complacency is real? Complacency walked in, charmed you with the scent of Drakkar Noir, and this fancy three-part name: highest individual potential.

HIGHEST INDIVIDUAL POTENTIAL (H.I.P)

You should agree with me about this because my perspective was earned...the hard way. Before I was embarrassed hearing the outstanding accomplishments of some of my former students, I was a cheerleader for highest individual potential. I was on the dance squad for it. I was doing fundraisers and telethons for H.I.P.! Yes, I even had a damn acronym for it! I was all in! That is until I heard from Ashleigh, who is now a teacher in Maryland. Humbly, she reached out to thank me for the work I'm doing today, and inspiring her when she was a fourth-grade student in my class. It was so great to hear from her that I arranged to speak with her speak by phone.

Our conversation eventually led to me asking about her career. I'll sum up our conversation this way. I found myself taking notes about education, educators, and our practice. And she was *just talking shop*, not trying to impress me or prove anything to me. To be clear, I never consciously applied limiting labels or expectations when I taught her as a fourth grader. At the same time, I didn't picture myself taking notes from a future excellent educator either.

Talking with Ashleigh has me reflecting about students I may have applied the highest individual potential lens to, and how I'm certain some of my students exceeded the highest individual potential expectations I had *for them*. And what scared me most is that I could've placed a ceiling above their heads with that mindset and prevented some of them from flourishing and being the best version of themselves. I never let my judgments skew my overall practice, but the fact that I had tried to guess at what their full potential was makes me shudder more than twenty-five years later.

Now, when I hear educators speak about helping students reach their H.I.P, I place them in the shoes of their students and have them experience the *low expectations of highest individual potential.* This experience taught me that our job as educators isn't to *predict* the future of our students, but to *provide* opportunities for students to *design* their future.

NATURAL ACCELERATION

When students are performing below grade-level, the typical response is to remediate and slow things down. But because The Crown represents grade-level or better, there must be a shift in your thinking. Growing students to the crown requires you to become more nimble, efficient, and urgent to accelerate their learning. You may find that there isn't time to make up every learning target. So, starting with student's strengths, you'll evaluate which targets have the most leverage; or bang for the buck. The goal is to identify the most efficient path to standard or better.

New and veteran educators alike report back how they tap into wells of creativity, innovation, and efficiency that they had no idea existed within them. They emerge from these cycles more decisive, more skilled, more confident, and best of all, ruthless.

YOUR STUDENTS OF COLOR DON'T NEED YOU TO KNOW RAP MUSIC; THEY NEED YOU TO TEACH LIKE THEY'RE GIFTED.

YOU HAVE TO KNOW BETTER FOR THEM

If you are a parent of a middle school aged child, I'm about to be "on your street." I'm talking about the child you *love* but sometimes don't *like* every day. The child who sprouted a few hairs here and there and now believes he's grown and has all the answers to life.

You know that person, right? Yes, you do. They think they have all of life figured out, but you, with your wisdom and experience, can see around corners they can't see. You know disaster awaits, and as a result, you have to make tough decisions as a parent. You have to *know better for them.* They may not be happy about your decision, but you know you're right.

When students make the poor choice to opt out of essential learning, you have to *know better for them.* Establishing systems, supports, boundaries, and expectations to help them navigate responsibility is part of our work. When a student at the elementary level requires extra time and support to master learning, you don't present the option to get support and then leave them to decide whether or not take it; you direct their steps to receive the support. The support built into the schedule to ensure they have access to it.

At the middle level, this approach continues, but not often with the directive approach. Students are sometimes given the *opportunity* to access needed support. They can choose to receive the support or not. This is a slippery slope that becomes more slippery at the high school level. Adults knowing better for students is routine practice at the elementary level. At the middle school level, we sometimes give too much credit to student growth spurts. We believe students should know better. Our thinking is, their choice to opt out will lead to them learning hard lessons through natural consequences. This *life lesson* approach applies in some circumstances, but it's too much of a risk regarding a students' education. There exists a sink-or-swim mindset on many campuses. The old school of thought was that negative consequences would teach students to be responsible, but it rarely turns out that way. Too often, students are left to choose whether to access additional support. And when students choose not to go for academic help, failure can be easily explained because support was available and students elected not to avail themselves to it. While we may be frustrated with their choices, we find a way to sleep at night by blaming *them* for not making the choice to get help. Does this scenario sound familiar?

The same thinking used with elementary students and your own child(ren) must be applied at all three levels. Even through high school, we have to know better for them. When we make this clear to students, we reconnect with what brought us to education: our mission to shape the future by ensuring learning. Complacency has infiltrated our profession with misaligned priorities such as ranking, sorting, and selecting students. We've moved away from ensuring learning and have gotten caught up in *sifting* students. If the two paths before the students we serve are to *sink or swim*, let's commit to teaching them to swim. My friend and colleague Doug Reeves captured the core of this principle in a way that changed my practice *and* my parenting. He said, "In life, consequence for not *doing the work,* is *doing the work.* He's right, and that mantra has guided me ever since.

THREE INHERENT TRUTHS ABOUT LEARNING

In her book, *The Pedagogy of Confidence*, Dr. Yvette Jackson outlined three inherent truths about learning. With a team of colleagues, share and discuss your thoughts about how each truth impacts your practice:

1. All people have an intrinsic desire to learn and to be self-actualized. Hierarchy of Needs psychologist Abraham Maslow has shown that this desire is the human imperative.

2. All brains are the same color. In other words, the way the brain makes learning happen doesn't differ from one culture to another.

3. All brains require the enrichment opportunities to demonstrate and build strengths, the supports to address weaknesses, the strategies for developing critical thinking, and the experiences that build the dispositions needed to be focused, engaged, tenacious and self-confident, and self-actualized.

COMPLACENCY IS ROOTED IN DEFICIT VOCABULARY

I invite you to think of a student currently working below grade-level. A student you'd describe as a "struggling learner." Write the student's name in the space below.

Student name_____

Now, list the student's top three strengths/gifts:

1. ....

2. ....

3. ....

How long did it take you to come up with three strengths/gifts? When you review your list, do any of your choices sound like a stretch?

....

....

....

In my professional learning experiences, I'll invite educators to partner up and share each student's three greatest strengths/gifts. The awkwardness that follows is obvious. The stalling, stammering, and nervous laughter are cringeworthy. I engage educators in this experience in order to create awareness. Our thinking about "struggling learners" focuses on deficits and not their strengths. It calibrates our expectations downward. This paradigm is especially true in underperforming schools, many located in urban areas. The word *urban* in the context of schools has taken on more meaning than describing the landscape.

"I have worked with many school districts in America where 'urban' is a euphemism used to refer to low-performing students of color and their educators, who are assumed to need their instruction scripted in order to increase student performance.

In these districts, administrators frantically search for a magic program that will save them from the penalties imposed as a result of the low performance on standardized tests of many of their students of color, a situation branded with the pernicious label, 'achievement gap.' The label has exacerbated the cultural myth that the only way to close the gap is by focusing on weaknesses. As a result, we have been obsessively misdirected to turn our backs on the vast intellectual capacity of these students and to regard minimum proficiency as the ceiling."

—Dr. Yvette Jackson

Human beings improve underdeveloped areas by leveraging strengths. Bathing students in underdeveloped areas kills the love of learning, and it also grinds the life out of educators. So often, strategies and practices intended to improve learning for students are ineffective because they focus solely on underdeveloped areas, and not student strengths. The recommended practices lack engagement, creativity, and rigor. Conversely, the most engaging, innovative, and creative practices are reserved for students performing at proficient or better levels. This serves only to widen the equity gap. We get better results when we are intentional about discovering the strengths and gifts within every student. Then we can empower them to leverage strengths and gifts in the service of improving underdeveloped areas.

Struggling Learner

Guiding Question: How would you feel if you were labeled as a "struggling learner" in a professional learning setting?

PRESSURE COAL TO CREATE DIAMONDS

The most effective educators you know are on an unceasing quest to un-leash the gifts that lie within each student, not just the students identified as "gifted." You know each of your students possesses unique strengths and gifts. Some students walk in with their gifts on display, looking like gleaming diamonds. Other students walk in with their gifts suppressed, atrophied, undiscovered, or unrealized, like coal buried in a mine. Students need you to put pressure on that coal so diamonds can emerge.

This work starts with defying the somatic markers that tell us only certain students possess gifts. We have to defy the notion that giftedness is limited to the narrow sliver of students identified by your district's inequitable and narrow assessment. If you're not sure you believe all kids have gifts, begin your work with a single decision: to behave as if every student possesses gifts waiting to be unleashed. If you're already there with your beliefs, your work will begin with the decision to be ruthless in your consistency around mining for every student's gifts, including those students who seem to make it their life's work to hide their gifts from you, like Trevor.

Sara Hovden is the associate principal at Hazel Point Intermediate School in Marion, Iowa. The school serves 547 fifth and sixth grade students. Sara shares an account of discovering the gifts that lay deep within a very challenging new student, Trevor.

"Trevor is a new fifth grader to our building. The only information we had about his history was that Hazel Point was his fourth school in five years of schooling, and he had an IEP (individualized education plan). On the first day of school, he displayed some pretty aggressive behaviors; throwing things and lots of swearing, so since day one, he's spent time with me in some form on almost a daily basis. Over time his behavior escalated. He wasn't aggressive toward others, but in other ways such as:

- hiding in school lockers
- running from staff and hiding in various areas inside the school

- climbing a cabinet and hiding in ceiling spaces.
- barricading himself inside a classroom

Trevor is a very angry student."

"Most days he doesn't want to go to class, and says he hates everyone. As a result of his behavior, I'm in communication with his parents on almost a daily basis. The other day I had him in my office. In what's become a routine, I'm working to de-escalate him to a point where he can attend class and not be disruptive. In the middle of him explaining that he didn't want to go to class, something in my office caught his eye. He asked, "You still have those two new computer monitors that don't work?" I said, "Yes, I've had IT (instructional technology department) look at them and they can't figure out how to get them to work." Our district boasts a very skilled and capable team of instructional technology specialists, and they visited my office twice to get the monitors working with no success. From his seat in my office, and without examining the monitors, cables, or my laptop, Trevor looked up and said, "I can fix that right now." Again, we have a very capable IT department, so no part of me thought Trevor could make the monitor configuration work. But I did see his request as a possible incentive for him to modify his behavior. I said, "I'll make a deal with you, you go to class and stay all morning, and then you can come help me fix this." He responded, "Well, I can do it right now." I said, "No, go and stay in class all morning and actually do your work, and you can earn a pass back to my office to fix my monitors."

"He went to class and had a great morning! He got his work done and behaved appropriately. He earned a pass to my office. For me, the victory was him having a productive morning. Again, I didn't think he could actually fix my technology issue. Well, he took apart one of my monitors, and upon reassembly, connected the appropriate cables, set up and connected my new laptop, configured the second monitor and enabled an extended screen set-up. In other words, Trevor delivered on his promise. He got the new monitors to work! In ten minutes, this ten-year old accomplished what certified professionals had yet to accomplish during two separate visits. He got everything working, took his pass and returned to class. This kid is a master with technology! He loves taking things apart, and we learned that he does a lot of this at home. After seeing what he was capable of, we've gotten things to engage him related to circuits and other technology. Trevor now feels valued, seen, and smart!"

"Trevor's behavior isn't perfect, but vastly improved, so much so that we're going to soon designate him as one of our school's Tech Ninjas. The opportunities for him to share his gift has Trevor *lit up*! He's doing a much better job staying in class and getting work done. I mean he's still got a *death stare* that can burn a hole through you, but underneath that veneer, there's a technology whiz kid. I tell him all the time, Trev, you can have a bright future in technology; you keep working at it! I love finding gifts in kids. Trevor is one of my most challenging students and one of my favorites. I see each day as another opportunity to try and figure him out."

Sara is ruthless about leveraging Trevor's strengths to deepen his sense of belonging, and be the best version of himself.

KIDS AND ADULTS

WE DON'T HAVE GOOD KIDS.
WE DON'T HAVE BAD KIDS...WE HAVE KIDS.
ALL KIDS MAKE GOOD AND POOR CHOICES.

WE DON'T HAVE GOOD ADULTS.
WE DON'T HAVE BAD ADULTS...WE HAVE ADULTS.
ALL ADULTS MAKE GOOD AND POOR CHOICES.

PRODUCTIVE STRUGGLE

Jen McCracken is ruthless. She serves as the Freshman Academy Principal at STEM High School in Akron, Ohio. Her district, Akron Public Schools, has taken a *low-floor, high-ceiling* approach to their math classes. This is revolutionary because math is often the content area rife with ability grouping and tracking. Here's how she explains it:

"Every student receives on-grade-level core instruction. It requires really knowing our learners; their strengths and weaknesses regarding each standard. During the planning phase, we anticipate any misconceptions or questions that may arise, as well as different ways our learners will solve problems. Once we have that sketched out, we create scaffolded assignments. We consider questions like: Using what our learners know, what can we give them to help them grow, without making them so frustrated that they give up? The goal is to engage them in productive struggle. Starting with what they know, we challenge them to push themselves to keep increasing their knowledge. Our mission is to move every student to mastery at grade-level or better, and this approach has been successful!" *This is Ruthless Equity in practice.* Many schools will take the same students and create more "low groups." *That is Complacency in practice.*"

Jen and the equity warriors of Akron Public Schools are reversing this trend. They are approaching mathematics instruction and expectations with Ruthless Equity.

PLC = PROFESSIONAL LEARNING CONFUSION

The most common example of ambiguity I see is the lack of understanding of the PLC (professional learning communities) process. School after school claims to be committed to the PLC process. My dialogue with the principal or other educator tends to go a lot like this:

- Principal: "We've been doing the PLC process for several years."

- Me: "That's awesome! As evidenced by what?"

- Principal: "Great! Our PLCs are awesome!"

- Me: "Fantastic! Tell me more. As evidenced by what?"

- Principal: "I'm glad you asked! Here's what we're doing:
    - Norms have been established on every team.
    - Collaborative teams meet on a weekly basis.
    - Time has been set aside for intervention.
    - We've got S.M.A.R.T. Goals!
    - Teams complete an agenda every week.
    - Our teams look at data.
    - We are data-driven.... We're all about the data."
    - We attended a PLC conference.

While that response cites several critical PLC components, none provide evidence of PLC effectiveness.

With a team of colleagues, discuss the following question.

What's missing from this principal's "evidence of effectiveness" list?

Now let's boil PLC outcomes down to their simplest forms. Revisit the "evidence of effectiveness" question. If you answered, data showing students' mastery of essential learning outcomes, then you get to grab a treat from the prize box!

PLC: ORGANIZING TO ENSURE EVERY STUDENT MASTERS ESSENTIAL LEARNING OUTCOMES.

That's it. It's that simple. At this moment, either the clouds just opened up in your world, or you are complete disbelief about how simple the definition is. With this simplified definition of PLCs, scroll up and take a second look at the list of answers the principal offered as evidence of effectiveness? Do any one of them provide evidence of effectiveness? No, they don't.

PLCs and Chicken

Guiding Question: What evidence does your team/school use to determine the effectiveness of PLCs?

PLC work boils down to monitoring every student's mastery of essential skills and competencies. The outcome of a PLC is measured by determining how close you are to one-hundred percent of your students mastering essential learning outcomes. That's all. Pretty black and white, right? It's so black and white, that the crystal-clear accountability of PLCs becomes scary for many. As a result, we cloud clarity by making "activity" our results instead of evidence of students mastering essential learning outcomes. Schools often make the *execution* of practice the measure of accountability instead of the *results* of the practice. This type of ambiguity provides a soft exit from accountability for student learning results. It numbs us into believing we're doing the right work, and helps us sleep easier. We have to be accountable for both the system and the results.

The opposite of ambiguity is clarity. PLC work has clear, measurable, and actionable outcomes. What are the essential outcomes? Did every student master them? If not, how are we going to make mastery happen? If so, how will we extend and enrich students who've mastered the outcome before others?

LIFE DOES NOT LEVEL DOWN

If your doctor misdiagnoses your symptoms and prescribes the wrong medicine, which results in your condition worsening, would you accept the excuse that your doctor was raised in a single-parent household where his mom worked three jobs? No, you wouldn't because:

LIFE DOES NOT LEVEL DOWN.

If your auto mechanic pours engine oil into the receptacle where your brake fluid should go, would you accept the excuse that he was in the low reading group in fourth grade? No, you wouldn't because:

LIFE DOES NOT LEVEL DOWN.

If your favorite coffee recipe calls for sugar, and salt is used instead, would you accept the excuse that the barista had an IEP (individualized education plan) back when he was in middle school? No, you wouldn't because:

LIFE DOES NOT LEVEL DOWN.

Creating ability groups and low tracks doesn't prepare students for real life. We are the profession that creates all professions. We must stop leveling down in schools.

HOW DO YOU ADDRESS THE NEEDS OF YOUR UNGIFTED LEARNERS?

For some, the question elicits the clutching of pearls, "How dare you ask that question? We don't refer to *any* of our students as ungifted!" I know, I know, no one uses the label, ungifted. But if your school has labeled a small percentage of students as "gifted," then it follows that all of your remaining students are "ungifted."

And while I'm back in your kitchen, allow me to knock a pot off the stove: I don't care what you tell your "ungifted students" once the "gifted kids" get picked up by your gifted teacher to do engaging work—you have sent them the clear message that they are *less than*, not as smart, and ungifted. And nothing you say, no poster you hang, no promised extra recess, "super student bucks," "you're awesome" stickers, or ice cream party can undo that thinking. Imagine attending professional learning I was facilitating. At the start of the workshop, I identify fifteen percent of the teachers in the session as gifted. I then provide them with an "enriched version of the content" that *you* won't have access to. Try telling me you won't be "in your feelings" about that. Would I get the best version of you during that workshop?

Brian Butler is a former school leader and nationally recognized thought leader around PLCs and equity. His recent blog provides powerful thoughts around exclusionary and inequitable gifted policies and practices. He stretched my thinking around the issue. I was focused on installing a wider figurative door so more students could have access to gifted services, and then Brian took a jackhammer to my foundation and cracked it wide open.

YOU'RE ASKING THE WRONG QUESTION

Here are excerpts from Butler's blog, *Access Creates Equity: Cultivating the Gifts of All Students*. Part I is entitled: "Asking the Right Questions?"

I am going to begin this blog with a challenge. My challenge to you is to wipe the slate clean and to be open to viewing "gifted education" through new eyes. This new way of thinking and doing would have gifted education as our floor, accessible to all and not just a select fortunate few.

All students have the capacity for high intellectual performance. We've just turned a blind eye to it, ignored it, or just outright have disregarded the research. The traditional idea of gifted education has supported this myth of the bell-shaped curve, supremacy, and a caste system in our schools. We have continued to ask the wrong questions regarding gifted education. The question we continue to ask is, "How do we qualify more students of color, school-dependent students, and English-language learners into gifted programs?" That's the wrong question! The question we should be asking is, how do we create the conditions, belief, and the mindset that all schools can give each student a gifted education? How can we awaken and cultivate the genius in *every single child*?

A team's collective efficacy and collective responsibility for every student will ensure a gifted experience for child. It will take fearless belief, expectations, and confidence from each educator to pull this off!

Can you see why Brian Butler rocked my foundation?

RUTHLESS REMINDERS

- Ruthless Equity educators "Start with The CROWN, *not with the kid*."
- Complacency thrives on the bell-shaped *curse* and the innate-ability paradigm.
- Any student expected to be a financially independent, productive member of our society must be taught at grade-level or higher.
- Beware the low expectations of highest individual potential.
- Teach to the highest level of every standard, and scaffold as appropriate.
- The more ambiguous you are, the less accountable you have to be.
- Life does not level down.
- Make the enrichment approach to gifted education the floor of every classroom; accessible to all learners.

DISRUPTIVE ACTION TO TAKE

With a team of colleagues, discuss the following questions.

Within this chapter, which ideas stand out?

How are you reacting to this information?

What adjustments in practice do you need to make in order to "Start with The Crown, not with the kid?"

CHAPTER EIGHT
THE FOURTH RULE OF RUTHLESSNESS
A COMMITMENT TO: MOMENTUM OVER MOOD RINGS

ENSURING EQUITY REQUIRES CONSISTENT RIGHT ACTION.
CONSISTENCY AND MOMENTUM ARE THE
LIFEBLOOD OF RUTHLESS EQUITY.
DEVELOP A DETACHMENT FROM
COMPLACENCY'S MANY DISTRACTIONS
SEEKING TO STOP YOU FROM CREATING LEARNING
BREAKTHROUGHS WITH YOUR STUDENTS.

THE RUTHLESS ARE NOT RULED BY MOOD RINGS

Your morning alarm goes off, escorting you out of a dream that left you smiling from ear to ear. You get out of bed to shower. You grab a pair of slacks you haven't worn in months, put them on, reach into your left pocket and find $45.

TODAY IS A GOOD DAY.

Your cream of wheat doesn't have a single lump in it, and on the way to work, the typical Sunday drivers know it's Monday morning. Every traffic light sees you coming, winks at you, and turns green as you approach. With a glance in your rear-view mirror you see your colleague, Brianna in the car behind you. Brianna likes to park her car in *your* parking space. No one has designated parking spaces, but everyone knows which parking space is yours! Brianna knows damn well too; but she likes to *try you*. Brianna got caught at the light, so she won't get your spot today!

TODAY IS A GOOD DAY.

On days like this you look down at your mood ring, and it's sky blue, baby! You're feeling good! You're greeting every colleague and student as they pass, even the ones who get on your nerves and make you want to "lay hands on them." This is shaping up to be a great day! You think to yourself, "Give me a bowl of Ruthless Equity with a side of high-expectations because...

TODAY IS A GOOD DAY.

But what about those other days? The days when your alarm clock goes off at the very moment the mayor hands you the cash winnings for the scratch-off ticket you didn't buy. When you get out of bed and your baby toe finds the corner of your nightstand before it finds your slipper. When you're running late, catching every red light, and Brianna is in the car in front of you. She makes it past the light that caught you, leaving you to watch her slide into your parking spot. You're seething. Your mood ring is dark blue, and the reading shows...

STAY OUT OF MY WAY TODAY.

This type of day happens to all of us, and when you're operating with Ruthless Equity, you must discipline yourself to overcome it. You have to stay outcome-focused. While you cannot always control circumstances around you, ruthlessness is understanding that **you are always in control of your response, behavior and choices.** When you're ruthless about creating an environment that makes students feel welcomed, valued, and seen, your demeanor can't be dictated by your mood ring. You must ascend to a higher plateau, driven by purpose.

Imagine for a moment that every service provider you encountered had license to operate based on their mood in the moment or on *whatever* challenges were happening in their life. Remember the bag draggers from earlier? How miserable would life be if everyone became a level 5 bag-dragger? Do you know why everyone doesn't operate this way? It's because to run a business, provide a service, or sell a product successfully, you've got to deliver the kind of service that keeps people coming back. Why? Because the customers are adults who have recourse. If you're mistreated, you have recourse; multiple avenues to provide feedback or rectify the situation.

You can lodge a complaint with management, contact the corporate office, post your grievance on social media or a review site, or decide to no longer patronize the business. When "less than our best" occurs in schools, students have little to no recourse. And delivering on the promise of equity for all students takes a back seat to disrupting the comfort of adults and challenging the status-quo.

The "what's best for adults first" lens exists because it's the path of least resistance; in other words, *we can get away with it.* We all know that given the choice of whether to confront a colleague about their behaviors toward students or ignore it, it's easier to maintain the status-quo than it is to hold adults accountable to the collective commitments of our shared mission.

Cheating students is easier than *challenging* adults. By and large, students don't request a meeting with the principal or superintendent to voice their concerns. Instead, "they cope." Our work demands an extra layer of moral imperative.

There are educators at your school who greet students with warmth and promise every day. We have to remember that hell breaks loose at times in their lives too. The difference is, they are ruthless about *being present*. They're firmly rooted in the present moment, and are guided by the light of the shared mission, not their mood ring.

The Ruthless Are Not Ruled By Mood Rings

Guiding Question: How will you become more consistent *(regardless of mood)* in your pursuit of equity?

DIPLEMENTATION

Every time you engage in new learning, new practices, new thinking that involves a learning curve, there's a *learning dip*, around the bend, awaiting your *fall*. You start the new learning journey with excitement and anticipation, and then at some point, you hit a learning curve. Learning curves can be frustrating and discouraging. They can knock you from the top of the mountain, where you stood full of hope, into the abyss, where you may question if the new learning is worth the frustration.

One of my leadership mentors, Ellie DeYoung, refers to this as "diplementation," a cool play on the notion of the implementation dip. We embrace diplementation intellectually, but the reality of it sometimes results in inconsistent implementation, or abandoning the initiative altogether.

Ruthless Equity in mindset and practice aren't exempt from this possibility. Rewiring of the brain in any form requires consistent repetition. Turning the corner with any new practice requires you to be both *consistent* and *persistent*. There's a fine line between not seeing the results you expect and continuing to forge ahead. We navigate diplementation effectively when we commit to a three-step process:

1. **Reflect:** Have you given the new learning enough time to take root? Are you experiencing challenges because you missed a step in the process?

2. **Regroup:** If the new learning requires more time and repetition, commit to continued, consistent implementation with an eye on the first sign of a breakthrough.

3. **Re-engage:** Continue to focus on *your* improvement around these new systems, policies, and practices. Don't become discouraged with early rollercoaster results. Embrace early inconsistency as part of the learning process.

This work is about *your* growth and improvement—the kind of improvement that leads to improved student learning.

THE SEDUCTION OF INSTANT GRATIFICATION

Would you abandon a new workout program after two days because you looked in the mirror and failed to see significant change? If you're serious about fitness goals, probably not. You know results take time. Unfortunately, this reality is absent in much of the messaging in today's society. We are bombarded with marketing that promises instant results. The world has come to worship the seduction of immediate gratification. Watch commercials, and you'll see what I mean: You'll see ones that claim you can buy *this* car with no money down, bad credit, no savings, and no job! Instant gratification weakens our constitution. Don't fall prey to Complacency trying to sell you this fragranced snake oil. When you become ruthless, you decide to show up to the gym, and work out consistently. The ruthless educator understands that the win lies just beneath the consistent application of mindset *and* practice. When you focus on improving these two areas, results will take care of themselves.

COMPLACENCY DOUBLES DOWN JUST WHEN YOU'RE READY TO QUIT

How many times have you found yourself frustrated because the breakthrough you need feels so far off? The span of the bridge you're building to move students to high levels of learning seems untenable. With reluctance, you're about to conclude that everything that could be done has been done. This is the moment when Complacency takes a swig of adrenaline smoothie and makes its hardest charge. You're tired and leaning against the ropes of the boxing ring. And Complacency winds up to hit you with everything it's got.

Why does Complacency throw its haymaker punch when you're feeling most discouraged? You see, Complacency knows what you don't: that your breakthrough is within reach. It knows your solution is just around the corner. It knows your team is close to cracking the code so it goes for the knockout!

When you become ruthless, you'll see this hard charge as a sign that you're close. You'll dig a little deeper and persist for a little longer. Learn to recognize the signs, because this time, more than any other, is when you must continue to act. Compounding this challenge is when negative student behaviors compound the issue and provide you with an additional layer of discouragement. I was there many times as a classroom teacher, and of all those experiences, my work as a 5th grade teacher with David stands out more than others.

David hated authority. He wouldn't do his work. He swore in class. He was one of the most difficult students to work with, and teachers couldn't get rid of him fast enough. David was known throughout the school. Saying his name in the staff lounge would make the lights flicker. Admittedly, my optimism and outlook were both challenged when I saw his name on my class roster. Despite that, I went into the new school year with positive intentions. I'm a relational teacher and sought to balance both connection and boundaries. When it came to intervening in David's behavior, I warned him, clarified expectations, and embedded positive reinforcements. His negative behaviors persisted. I decided to spend some one-on-one time with him and talk, man to *young* man.

We talked for about 30 minutes. He told me that he hated school, hated going home, and didn't have any friends. He didn't trust me and had no plans to explore the prospect of a relationship. He gave me the student *stiff-arm*. A stiff arm is a move in football, where the ball carrier extends his arm to prevent defenders from gaining a firm hold on his body and tackling him. Intellectually, I knew David was pushing me away because he's used to people becoming worn down and giving up on him. I understood this and admit that his persistent stiff-arm proved effective over time. He was ruthless about fending me off, and there were a few days when I wished he didn't show up. Fortunately, there were many more days when I wanted him to show up so I could figure out how break down his barrier.

Days after our talk, David earned a two-day suspension for giving the "one finger salute" to another teacher. I was crushed and angry. I was crushed because my efforts felt like I was pushing Jell-O uphill. I was angry because David doesn't see that I care for him. I felt guilty because there were moments when felt aligned with other teachers who were fed up and had enough of his antics.

While David was *never* absent from school, he did mention that his home life is chaotic. His mom wouldn't wake him up for school. She wouldn't sign permission slips for field trips and activities. His home was a revolving door of relatives living there temporarily, and men romantically involved with his mother moving in and out of the apartment. The more I learned, the more I concluded that school was probably the most stable place in his life. And, the adults at school were probably the most stable people in his life. David needed to be in school. And I needed to do my part so David experienced the support and stability I just described.

His return to school showed no signs of lessons learned. I could see his behavior escalating. He was auditioning for another out-of-school-suspension. During one of our one-to-one meetings, exasperated, he asked, Why do you keep trying to help me? Can't you see that I don't have anything going for me?" Tell me why you don't have anything going for you. "Well, I'm dumb. I can't read and I can't do math. I'm in special ed and to go to classes with other slow kids. I don't get why you want to talk with me all the time. Why do you keep asking me questions like I'm smart?" "David, my job is to reach inside and bring out the best version of you. Your teachers need to see that version of you, your classmates need to see that version of you, and most importantly, you need to see that version of you. He's in there, and like it or not, I'm not going to stop searching until I find him. That's my job. You can make my job easy or difficult, but young man, it's getting done. I'm not going anywhere!"

His next question floored me. "All of my other teachers have always given up by now. Why haven't you?" I responded with a sense of deep empathy and urgency. Up until now, David hid behind his anger and inappropriate sense of humor. "Because, David, I care about how you feel when you're here. I know what you need to be successful in school and in life. I care if you're having a good day and want to know how I can help you when you're having a bad day. I want school to be a place where the good feeling you have on a Tuesday makes you want to come back on Wednesday. Part of that process is letting you know that there is someone here you can count on. That someone you can count on is me."

We talked more. I opened my desk drawer and grabbed the language arts honors medal I earned in second grade. I told David about my teacher, Sister Mary Claire, and how she had an amazing way of making me feel like I mattered. And how decades later, I keep that medal in my desk drawer as a reminder of what she did for me, and how I'm driven to pay it forward with him. He listened skeptically. He probably thought

I was making up this story, and picked up the medal at the dollar store. That is until I turned the medal over and showed him the inscription on the back, K. Williams '75. He was a believer at that point.

As the bell rang and dismissal began, David was making his way to his bus. In a moment, he turned back, walked over to me, and gave me a hug; a display of positive, warm affection from the very student that every other teacher warned me about. I had been working tirelessly with David all year. And there were several times when I wanted to just give up on him. The time we spent talking today didn't have magic. I believe the breakthrough was a culmination of countless times when I endured David's stiff arm and kept returning to the huddle for the next play. Just as I was considering giving up, we finally made a breakthrough.

My daily interaction with David made him feel seen, and gave him a sense of belonging. David's educational and social gains were prominent on the list of highlights of that year. Before I met David, he was learning with 2nd and 3rd graders in a self-contained special education setting and reading at a 1st grade-level. By April, his reading had advanced by almost two grade-levels, and he was working independently in math at grade-level.

My experience with David made me more intentional about knowing my students on a more personal level and discovering each students' unique strengths. The experience I've gained teaching David has gifted me with the knowledge that I'm close to a breakthrough when things feel like they're breaking down.

THE ROAD TO RUTHLESS EQUITY IS LONG AND CHALLENGING;
YOU WILL BE DISCOURAGED, BUT WHEN YOU PERSEVERE, YOUR REWARDS
AND THE BENEFITS TO YOUR STUDENTS WILL BE IMMEASURABLE."
— DAVID HOGAN, MY RUTHLESS EDITOR

THE RUTHLESS FIGHT PROCRASTINATION

Procrastination is another form of Complacency. The blog you want to start, the business you'd like to launch, the book you plan to write, the exercise regimen you'll one day begin.

In schools, procrastination is more insidious. Rarely do educators say things like, "I'm not going to use that research-based data protocol that came so highly recommended because it feels really awkward to share and compare assessment results." Instead of saying that, things somehow get so busy during the meeting that we just kind of never get around to the protocol. Tons of activity can fool us into believing we're too busy and overwhelmed and can't get to the most important work. You can justify procrastination by making "frenzied activity," not "focused activity," the reason you put off engaging the right work.

YOU CAN'T SNEAK UP ON EQUITY

You Can't Sneak Up on Excellence.
You can't hope your way to excellence.
You can't talk your way to excellence.
You can't "book study" your way to excellence.
You can't Ted Talk your way to excellence.
You can't tiptoe your way to excellence.
You Can't Sneak Up on Equity.
You can't *probrecito* your way to equity.
You can't *bless his heart* your way to equity.
You can't *ability group* your way to equity.
You can't *dumb down* your way to equity.
You can't *sympathize* your way to equity.
You've got to **show up** differently.
You've got to be **ruthless**.

COMPLACENCY AND A FOCUS ON ACTIVITY

Complacency doesn't show itself as a school full of educators shopping on their phones while showing movies in class all day long. Complacency takes a more subtle and deceptive form: a lot of well-intentioned activity. The issue with teachers isn't effort and activity; the problem is when the culture shifts from evidence of student learning as the result to "activity" as the result. The complacent educator laments, "We're working as hard as we can!" This becomes a euphemism for "Don't you dare ask me to do anything else!" I can't blame educators who bang this drum. When activity is the result, there is no payoff, no score! Teachers need a payoff. When schools move from being *results*-oriented to *activity*-oriented, measurable results are no longer available to evaluate the effectiveness of our work. Over time, this wears teachers down and as a result, the stage is set for more Complacency.

RUTHLESS REMINDERS

- *Diplementation* is a part of every process that involves a learning curve. Expect it and embrace it when it arrives.
- Do not be *seduced* and *derailed* by short-term results.
- The key leveraging arm of improvement isn't with students, but with improving your *systems, practices,* and *protocols.*
- Commitment to maintaining momentum in the face of a cloudy mood ring.
- Complacency turns up the heat when you're about to give up.
- Keep student learning results at the center of your work.
- Pursue the right outcomes of a PLC; mastery of essential learning outcomes.
- Don't allow students to opt out of essential work. *Know better for them,* and create systems that "harass 'em 'till they pass (with love)."

DISRUPTIVE ACTION TO TAKE

With a team of colleagues, discuss the following questions.

Within this chapter, what ideas *stand out*?

When, in your personal life have you applied the Ruthless Rule, Momentum Over Mood Rings?

How will you embed Momentum Over Mood Rings in your Ruthless Equity practice?

CHAPTER NINE
YOU MUST DE-CIDE

UNTIL ONE IS COMMITTED, THERE IS HESITANCY, THE CHANCE TO DRAW BACK, ALWAYS INEFFECTIVENESS. CONCERNING ALL ACTS OF INITIATIVE (AND CREATION), THERE IS ONE ELEMENTARY TRUTH, THE IGNORANCE OF WHICH KILLS COUNTLESS IDEAS AND SPLENDID PLANS: THAT THE MOMENT ONE DEFINITELY COMMITS ONESELF, THEN PROVIDENCE MOVES TOO. ALL SORTS OF THINGS OCCUR TO HELP ONE THAT WOULD NEVER OTHERWISE HAVE OCCURRED. A WHOLE STREAM OF EVENTS ISSUES FROM THE DECISION, RAISING IN ONE'S FAVOUR ALL MANNER OF UNFORESEEN INCIDENTS AND MEETINGS AND MATERIAL ASSISTANCE, WHICH NO MAN COULD HAVE DREAMT WOULD HAVE COME HIS WAY.
—W. H. MURRAY, SCOTTISH MOUNTAINEER AND WRITER

DE-CIDE

Consider the word *decide.* What do the words:

- Pesticide
- Suicide
- Insecticide
- Homicide

have in common? They all end with *cide,* which connotes death. So, taken directly from the gospel according to Ruthless Equity, chapter 9, verse 1, when you *de-cide,* it means you've put ALL other options to *death.*

DECIDE (DE-CIDE): TO PUT ALL OTHER OPTIONS TO DEATH.

Let this definition wash over you. From this moment forward, live and work with this definition in mind. When you "de-cide" to teach with Ruthless Equity, you put all other options to death. This means you turn your back on communicating any other way. You turn your back on dealing with colleagues any other way. The door behind you locks forever, and you only align with factors within your sphere of influence that advance the mission of equity for all. You stand guard and protect this approach while others around you continue to navigate the fears and distractions of Complacency. Illuminate the way for them.

The commitment to Ruthless Equity is a life-altering decision. Your decision will stand with others you've made after growing tired of disappointments, false starts, giving into fear, hitting the wall, and getting kicked in the teeth over and over again. Once you de-cide, there is no going back. If you decide to take this powerful step, I promise that you'll look back on this moment as career turning point.

COMPLACENCY OBSTRUCTS ONLY WHEN YOU REACH UPWARD

Complacency seeks to obstruct when you are reaching in the direction of learning for all. It obstructs when reaching for higher levels of student learning and educator efficacy. Complacency shows up when you decide students need multiple opportunities to demonstrate mastery. It shows up when you stretch beyond your comfort zone. It arrives when you dare to see more in students than they see in themselves; when you dare see beyond marginalizing labels. Complacency sees that you've shown up to the party, not with stories about how you've done all you can, but in search of one more idea or suggestion to try. As you approach the door to enter the party, Complacency is on the other side trying to keep you out.

WHO SAW MORE IN YOU?

I'm going to end this book where it started. Early on, I shared my experience with two teachers who saw more in me than I saw in myself. When I consider this question as an adult, I can identify people in each decade of my life who looked *through* me and saw more in me than I saw in myself.

These handful of people occupy the mantle of my soul. *I am* because of *who they are*. They spoke greatness into me. They challenged me to stretch beyond my comfort zone. They suggested I do things I never thought I could, including sitting down to write *this* book. They challenged me to become more than I ever dreamed I could be.

At times, I was exhilarated by their expectations, and at other times, doubted them at every turn. I was scared to death by the CROWN they challenged me to grow tall enough to wear. I couldn't see what they saw, but the power of these connections sustained me while I navigated my own doubts and fears. I couldn't turn away from their vision because I couldn't let them down. And while "not letting someone down" isn't the most authentic way to move forward, it was effective because once I broke through my own barriers and saw results, my moving forward became intrinsic. Now it's your turn.

Take a few moments to reflect and respond to the questions below:

Who saw more in you than you saw in yourself?

....

....

....

What did they challenge you to do?

....

....

....

Who did they challenge you to become?

....

....

....

What has been the result?

....

....

....

Ensuring high levels of learning for every student is an opportunity for you to become *that* educator for the students you serve. There's no application process and there's no interview. You have to show up and be ruthless. You have to be "on" all the time, because you'll not always know the moment you become an influencer in a student's life.

You're going to shatter old paradigms, policies, and practices like the innate ability paradigm, focusing on weaknesses, violations of dignity, ability-grouping, bias, and assumptions that have resulted in false narratives about your students. You will usher in new paradigms that compel you to set expectations based on agreed-upon essential learning outcomes and not student background and circumstance. You're going to shock some of your students with your high-expectations. Some will need time for their brains to be rewired. You'll allow for that as you grow them tall enough wear The Crown.

Over time, you'll be joined by legions of Ruthless Equity warriors who also shun marginalizing labels, inequitable practices, fixed-mind-set, and a lack of belonging and inclusion, and organize to move all students "to wear The Crown." Bringing things full circle, know that teaching with Ruthless Equity will transform you from an educator who once wondered, **can I make a difference** to an educator who now knows, **I am the difference!** Become ruthless and do what you were brought to this amazing profession to do!

THE WORLD IS CHANGED BY YOUR EXAMPLE, NOT YOUR OPINION. —PAUL COELHO, BRAZILIAN LYRICIST AND NOVELIST

RUTHLESS REMINDERS

- DE-CIDE means to put ALL other options to death.
- You cannot tiptoe into equitable practice; you've got to be "all in."
- Speak greatness into your students, trusting that you'll find the keys to unlock learning and unleash their greatness.
- See more in your students than they see in themselves, just as someone once saw more in you than you saw in yourself.
- If this book changed you for the better in any way, please recommend it to a colleague.

DISRUPTIVE ACTION TO TAKE

With a team of colleagues, discuss the following questions.

Recall a situation when you refused to accept the "low expectations" associated with a student.

Recall a situation when you made a decision, and put all other options to death. What stand did you take? What did you decide?

Share an example when you built a relationship with a student that led to learning breakthroughs and a stronger sense of belonging.

What habits of mind and practice did you *decide* to *stop doing* as a result of reading this book?

Which habits of **mind** did you add to your toolbox as a result of reading *Ruthless Equity*?

Which habits of **practice** did you add to your toolbox as a result of reading *Ruthless Equity*?

IT IS NOT THE CRITIC WHO COUNTS; NOT THE MAN WHO POINTS OUT HOW THE STRONG MAN STUMBLES, OR WHERE THE DOER OF DEEDS COULD HAVE DONE THEM BETTER. THE CREDIT BELONGS TO THE MAN WHO IS ACTUALLY IN THE ARENA, WHOSE FACE IS MARRED BY DUST AND SWEAT AND BLOOD; WHO STRIVES VALIANTLY; WHO ERRS, WHO COMES SHORT AGAIN AND AGAIN, BECAUSE THERE IS NO EFFORT WITHOUT ERROR AND SHORTCOMING; BUT WHO DOES ACTUALLY STRIVE TO DO THE DEEDS; WHO KNOWS GREAT ENTHUSIASMS, THE GREAT DEVOTIONS; WHO SPENDS HIMSELF IN A WORTHY CAUSE; WHO AT THE BEST KNOWS IN THE END THE TRIUMPH OF HIGH ACHIEVEMENT, AND WHO AT THE WORST, IF HE FAILS, AT LEAST FAILS WHILE DARING GREATLY, SO THAT HIS PLACE SHALL NEVER BE WITH THOSE COLD AND TIMID SOULS WHO NEITHER KNOW VICTORY NOR DEFEAT.
—THEODORE ROOSEVELT

ACKNOWLEDGMENTS

My wife Nicole and I raised our two kids to use the word, *challenge* instead of *hard,* because no one wants to do anything *hard*, but everyone loves a *challenge*. As young as three years old, they had to do push-ups if they used the word, *hard*. Well, I just did fifty push-ups because I'm here to tell you, writing this book was hard. It was harder than I thought and more rewarding than I could have ever imagined. None of this would have been possible without my family, my wife, Nicole, son, Adam and daughter Mia. They gifted me with valuable feedback, constant encouragement, and steadfast support during this rollercoaster of momentum and frustration, breakdowns and break-throughs, progress and false starts. I am grateful for their steadfast love and support.

I wrote this book because I believed I had something valuable to offer educators. When Dr. Anthony Muhammad reviewed an early draft of this book and agreed to write the foreword, it triggered an instant confidence boost I wasn't expecting. When I read the foreword he wrote, I was floored. It humbled me and assured me that I was onto something.

I'm grateful to Dr. Rick DuFour, Dr. Robert Eaker, Becky DuFour, and Jeff Jones for recognizing my work as a school leader almost fifteen years ago, and providing me with a platform and partnership that allowed me to learn, grow, and impact education nationally. Professional Learning Communities at Work is and always has been an equity initiative, and these mentors allowed me to use their voices until I found my own. God rest the souls of Rick and Becky DuFour.

The selfless generosity of educator and author, Dr. Chad Dumas led to him introducing me to my awesome publishing coach, Martha Bullen. I never considered publishing independently. I thought it to be intimidating and overwhelming. I was about to sign with a publisher, and Chad recommended that I meet with Martha first. I'm glad I did. Martha is knowledgeable about publishing, passionate about coaching authors through the process, and she broke down the process into bite-sized steps that convinced me I could do it. She assembled a phenomenal team that includes designer Christy Day and editor David Hogan. Like Ruthless Equity teachers, all three of them stretched me with high expectations with support. Working in concert with this awesome publishing team is my right hand; my executive assistant, Jessica Meeks. When your assistant is as invested in the success of your business as you are, you've struck gold. Jess is the glue behind the scenes that holds my company, Unfold The Soul together.

I love classic movies. After working with my book designer, Christy Day, I not only enjoy the movie, but also pay close attention to the font, layout, and design of movie posters and opening and closing credits. I do this because Christy Day has shown me the impact of cover design, page layout, and fonts. I'm grateful for her investment in this project, her patience with me, and the creativity of her work.

I wonder if my editor, David Hogan and I are related. His style of unvarnished and supportive feedback is exactly how I coach school teachers and leaders. He coached me like the family member who is unafraid to tell you what you *need to hear*, but might not *want to hear*. David edited *Ruthless Equity* this way. His unvarnished coaching has pushed me out of my comfort zone and made me a better writer and this a much better book.

Wish In One Hand Press would like to thank the following reviewers:

Justin Baeder, PhD, Author of *Now We're Talking! 21 Days to High-Performance Instructional Leadership*

Naomi Austin, EdS, Secondary Principal

Sanée Bell, Ed.D., Author, Speaker, Educational Thought Leader

Anisa Baker-Busby, Ed.D., Principal and Educational Consultant

Marcus L. Broadhead, Ed.D., Educational Leader, Author, Speaker

Bethany Brown, Principal, Buffalo Public Schools

Jessica Cabeen, Nationally Distinguished Principal, Author and Speaker

Luis F. Cruz, PhD., Author and Education Consultant

Dr. Chad Dumas, Author, *Let's Put the C in PLC: A Practical Guide for School Leaders*

Sean Daugherty, M. Ed., Kindergarten Teacher

John D. Ewald, Ed.D., Former Superintendent, Principal, Teacher

Kandace Friend, Third Grade Teacher

JoAnne Greear, Principal, Jenifer Middle School

Dr. William C. Greene, Jr. Principal

Keri Hughes, Classroom Teacher

Baruti Kafele, Educator, Retired Principal, Author

Brig Leane, Educational Consultant

Angela Maiers, Founder & CEO, Choose To Matter

Dr. Tom Many and Susan Sparks, Authors and Educational Consultants

Mike Mattos, Educator, Author, and Consultant

Krystalyn E. May, Fifth Grade Teacher, Lindsey Elementary School

Dr. Alison J. Mello, Assistant Superintendent and Author

Dr. Rosa Perez-Isiah, Author, Consultant, and Education Leader for Social Justice

Cory Radisch, Educator, Consultant, and co-host of The StatusGROW Podcast

Dr. Douglas Reeves, Author, *Achieving Equity and Excellence*

Georgina Rivera, K-8 School Administrator, NCSM 2nd Vice President

Eric Sheninger, Google Certified Innovator Adobe Education Leader

Dr. Jared Smith, Superintendent, Author, and Speaker

Dr. Felecia Spicer, Educational Leader

Jove Stickel, Principal Lafayette Co. C-1 Middle School

Dani Trimble, Superintendent, Alburnett School District

Michael Walker, Assistant Director/Teacher Center Coordinator Arkansas River Education Cooperative

BIBLIOGRAPHY

For their generous permission to quote from their works, the author acknowledges the following sources:

"The 5 Second Rule Summary." 12 Min Blog, 17 Mar. 2018, blog.12min.com/the-5-second-rule-summary/

Adams, Cecil. "To African-Americans, What DOES 'Signifying' Mean?" The Straight Dope, 28 Sept. 1984, www.straightdope.com/21341677/to-african-americans-what-does-signifying-mean

Admin. "From a Nation at Risk to a Nation at Hope." 14 Feb. 2019, nation-athope.org/report-from-the-nation/

Alternatives to Privatizing Public Education and Curriculum: Festschrift In, Routledge, 2019, pp. 74–74

Bailey, Kim and Chris Jakicic. *Simplifying Common Assessment: A Guide for Professional Learning Communities at Work*, Solution Tree Press, 2017, pp. 82–82

Berreby, David. "Emonomics." The New York Times, 16 Mar. 2008, https://www.nytimes.com/2008/03/16/books/review/Berreby-t.html

Buffum, Austin and Mike Mattos. *It's about Time: Planning Interventions and Extensions in Elementary School.* Solution Tree Press, 2015

Butler, Brian. "Access Creates Equity Cultivating The Gifts of All Students." Brian Butler—Educational Consultant, 27 Aug. 2021, www.brianbutler.info/post/access-creates-equity-cultivating-the-gifts-of-all-students

Carolla, Adam. "Rapper and Provocateur Zuby on COVID, Vaccines, and Human Nature." *The Adam Carolla Show*, 9 July 2021, adamcarolla.com/zuby-peter-north/. Accessed 15 July 2021

Clear, James. *Atomic Habits an Easy & Proven Way to Build Good Habits & Break Bad Ones.* Penguin Audio, an Imprint of the Penguin Random House Audio Publishing Group, 2019

Cobb, Floyd and John Krownapple. *Belonging Through a Culture of Dignity: The Keys to Successful Equity Implementation.* Mimi &Todd Press, Inc. Kindle Edition. 2019

"Complacency - Definition." merriam-webster.com/ https://www.merriam-webster.com/dictionary/complacency

Clagon, Keith. Dr. Lorraine Monroe on 60 Minutes, insolentpolitics.blogspot.com/2013/06/dr-lorraine-monroe-on-60-minutes.html. 2013

Clayton R. Cook, Aria Fiat, Madeline Larson, Christopher Daikos, Tal Slemrod, Elizabeth Holland, Andrew J. Theyer & Tyler Renshaw. "Positive greetings at the door: Evaluation of a low-cost, high-yield proactive classroom management strategy." *Journal of Positive Behavior Interventions,* 20(3), 149–159, 2018

Couros, George. *The Innovator's Mindset: Empower Learning, Unleash Talent, and Lead a Culture of Creativity.* Dave Burgess Consulting, 2015

"Crabs-in-a-Barrel." *Urban Dictionary* www.urbandictionary.com/define.php?term=crabs-in-a-barrel

Dobbin, Frank and Alexandra Kalev. "Are diversity programs merely ceremonial? Evidence-free institutionalization." *The SAGE Handbook of Organizational Institutionalism* (pp. 808–828) Sage. 2017

Dufour, Richard, et al. Learning by Doing: *A Handbook for Professional Learning Communities at Work.* Solution Tree Press, 2016

Evans, Margaret, Rebecca M. Teasdale, Nora Gannon-Slater, Priya G. La Londe, Hope L. Crenshaw, Jennifer C. Greene, & Thomas A. Schwandt. How did that happen? Teachers' explanations for low test scores. Teachers College Record, 121(2), 1–40. 2019

Formica, Michael J. "How Labels Limit Us and We, in Turn, Limit Our Own Potential." Psychology Today, Sussex Publishers, www.psychologytoday.com/us/blog/enlightened-living/200807/how-labels-limit-us-and-we-in-turn-limit-our-own-potential. 2008

"Frederick Douglass Declares There Is 'NO Progress Without Struggle' · SHEC: Resources for Teachers." *Social History for Every Classroom,* shec.ashp.cuny.edu/items/show/1245

Gay, Geneva. *Culturally responsive teaching: Theory, research, and practice.* New York, NY: Teachers College Press. 2010

Grammarist, grammarist.com/idiom/elephant-in-the-room/

Graves, Christopher. "Part One: 'We Are Not Thinking Machines. We Are Feeling Machines That Think." *Institute for Public Relations*, 13 Dec. 2020, isttuteforpr.org/part-one-not-thinking-machines-feeling-machines-think/#_ftn3

Hall, Roberta M., and Bernice R. Sandler. The classroom climate: A chilly one for women? https://files.eric.ed.gov/fulltext/ED215628.pdf 1982

Jackson, Yvette. *The Pedagogy of Confidence: Inspiring High Intellectual Performance in Urban Schools*, Hawker Brownlow Education, 2015, pp. 17–18

Jacobson, Sheri. "The Victim Mentality - What It Is and Why You Have It." *Harley Therapy™ Blog*, 26 Aug. 2021, www.harleytherapy.co.uk/counselling/victim-mentality.htm

Kanold, Timothy D. *Soul!: Fulfilling the Promise of Your Professional Life as a Teacher and Leader*. Solution Tree Press, 2021

Kidde Brand Carbon Monoxide Detectors. Online Instructional Manual. images.homedepot-static.com/catalog/pdfImages/8e/8e5f26df-97c1-47d1-8368-318243b9fd1f.pdf

Krownapple, John. "Belonging: The Missing Equity Ingredient." *The Core Collaborative*, 2 Dec. 2019, https://www.thecorecollaborative.com/post/belonging-the-missing-equity-ingredient

Ladson-Billings, Gloria. "But that's just good teaching! The case for culturally relevant pedagogy." *Theory into Practice*, 34(3), 159–165. 1995

"Leadership for Lean Manufacturing." Strategos Inc., www.strategosinc.com/leadership_relational.htm. 19 Nov. 2003

Liljedahl, Peter. "Visibly Random Groups." *Peterliljedahl.com*, https:/peterliljedahl.com/wp-content/uploads/Visibly-Random-Groups.pdf. 2014

Lindsey, Randall B., Laraine M. and Franklin Campbell Jones. *The culturally proficient school: An implementation guide for school leaders*. Corwin Press. 2013

Mattos, Mike. *Concise Answers to Frequently Asked Questions about Professional Learning Communities at Work,* Solution Tree Press, 2016

McRobbie, Michael A., et al. "The Return of Phineas Gage: Clues about the Brain from the Skull of a Famous Patient." *Science*, 20 May 1994, science.sciencemag.org/content/264/5162/1102

Muhammad, Anthony. *Overcoming the Achievement Gap Trap: Liberating Mindsets to Effect Change*. Solution Tree Press, 2015

Nollan, Jack. "8 Reasons You Feel like You Don't Belong Anywhere." *A Conscious Rethink*, 14 Oct. 2021, https://www.aconsciousrethink.com/7567/dont-belong/

Oakes, Jeannie. *"Public Scholarship: Education Research for a Diverse Democracy"* Educational Researcher, March 2018 (Vol. 47, #2, p. 91-104)

Pitler, Howard. "The New School Year: Six Questions to Ask Your Students on Day One." *Ed Circuit*, 7 Aug. 2017, www.edcircuit.com/new-school-year-six-questions-ask-students/

Pressfield, Steven. *The War of Art*, Black Irish Press, 2011, pp. 87–88

"A Quote by Theodore Roosevelt." Goodreads, www.goodreads.com/quotes/7-it-is-not-the-critic -who-counts-not-the-man

"A Quote by William Hutchison Murray." Goodreads, www.goodreads.com/quotes/1465306-until-one-is-committed-there-is-hesitancy-the-chance-to

Rivera, Georgina. "Mathematicians at Work, Expect Noise: A Conversation with Georgina Rivera." *Ed Reports*, 9 July 2021, www.edreports.org/resources/article/mathematicians-at-work-expect-noise-a-conversation-with -georgina-rivera

Rosenthal, Robert and & Lenore Jacobson. *Pygmalion in the classroom: Teacher expectation and pupils' intellectual development.* Rinehart and Winston. 1968

Smith, Dominique B.; Douglas Fisher, and Nancy Frey. *Removing Labels*, Grades K-12 (Corwin Literacy) (p. 214). SAGE Publications. Kindle Edition. 2021

Stöber, Joachim. "Self-Pity: Exploring the Links to Personality, Control Beliefs, and Anger." Wiley Online Library, John Wiley & Sons, Ltd, 14 Mar. 2003, onlinelibrary.wiley.com/doi/abs/10.1111/1467-6494.7102004

Student Handbook - Morehouse College. www.morehouse.edu/media/student-development/Morehouse-College---Student-Handbook---2019-2020.pdf

Williams, Kenneth C. and Tom Hierck. *Starting a Movement: Building Culture from the inside out in Professional Learning Communities.* Solution Tree Press, 2015

"The World Is Changed by Your Example, Not by Your Opinion." *Quote Fancy*, quotefancy.com/quote/384277/Paulo-Coelho-The-world-is-changed-by-your-example-not-by-your-opinion

ABOUT THE AUTHOR

KEN WILLIAMS is a husband, father, nationally-recognized trainer, speaker, coach and consultant in leadership and school culture. A practitioner for nearly three decades, Ken led the improvement efforts at two schools by leveraging the Professional Learning Communities at Work process. Through his company, Unfold The Soul, Ken is skilled in joining the *why* of the work to the *how* of the work. He is known for his powerful and engaging combinations of "heart, humor, and hammer." He is a status-quo disruptor, warm demander, and an unapologetic identifier of elephants in the room, with his lens firmly fixed on maximizing the collective strengths of educators in the service of equity and excellence for every student.

When not working, Ken is often out "running errands for no reason" in one of two vintage cars, his 1975 Oldsmobile Delta 88 Royale convertible or his 1972 Buick Riviera. He's an avid bowler, a lover of classic film, and old-school R&B music. The more of those he can do in a day, the better. He also derives joy from creating memories with family and friends. Ken was raised in Queens, New York and currently lives in Atlanta, Georgia with his wife, Nicole, son, Adam, daughter, Mia, and their dog, Murphy. For more information about Ken, scan the QR code below or visit Unfold The Soul at www.unfoldthesoul.com.

Made in the USA
Monee, IL
20 May 2022

96785155R00128